how to be
better at . . .

delegation and coaching

how to be
better at...

delegation and coaching

Tony Atherton

YOURS TO HAVE AND TO HOLD

BUT NOT TO COPY

First South Asian Edition 2000

Kogan Page India Private Limited
4325/3 Ansari Road
New Delhi 110 002.

This edition is for sale only in India, Bangladesh, Nepal, Pakistan and Sri Lanka only. Not for export elsewhere.

ISBN 81-7554-107-5

Rs. 135.00

Published by Vinod Vasishtha for Kogan Page India Private Limied, 4325/3 Ansari Road, Daryaganj, New Delhi 110 002, and printed at Raj Press, New Delhi.

CONTENTS

How to be a Better...series

Whether you are in a management position or aspiring to one, you are no doubt aware of the increasing need for self-improvement across a wide range of skills.

In recognition of this and sharing their commitment to management development at all levels, Kogan Page and the Industrial Society have joined forces to publish the How to be a Better...series.

Designed specifically with your needs in mind, the series covers all the core skills you need to make your mark as a high-performing and effective manager.

Enhanced by mini case studies and step-by-step guidance, the books in the series are written by acknowledged experts who impart their advice in a practical way which encourages effective action. Now you can bring your management skills up to scratch and give your career prospects a boost with the How to be a Better...series!

Titles available are:

How to be a Better...Communicator
How to be a Better...Creativity
How to be a Better...Customer Care
How to be a Better...Decision Maker
How to be a Better...Delegation and Coaching
How to be a Better...Giving Presentations
How to be a Better...Interviewer
How to be a Better...Managing Change
How to be a Better...Meetings
How to be a Better...Motivating People
How to be a Better...Negotiator
How to be a Better...Problem Solver
How to be a Better...Project Manager
How to be Better at writing...Reports & Proposals
How to be a Better...Teambuilder
How to be a Better...Time Manager

Available from all goods booksellers. For further information on the series, please contact:

Kogan Page India Private Limited
4325/3 Ansari Road, Daryaganj, New Delhi 110 002
Tel. : 3279280, 3283121, 3285874 Fax : 91-11-3267224

PREFACE

The purpose of this book is to help you to become better at delegation and coaching. The fact that you are reading it is an indication that you believe you can be better at these essential management skills.

Organizations of all shades have shed staff and reduced their levels of management in the last two decades or so. This process has inevitably put more pressure on fewer people to achieve the same results, or perhaps greater results. The outcome can be intolerable stress. However, if better management styles are adopted and if staff are coached, delegated to and empowered then productivity can be increased and stress controlled. The management skills of delegation and coaching have therefore grown in importance and look set to continue to grow in the future.

Regrettably, it is still true though that too many managers and supervisors act as if delegation is simply about telling people to do something and blaming them if it goes wrong, and that coaching is simply telling them more slowly and more loudly. Companies that encourage that type of behaviour are dinosaurs awaiting extinction and their management will one day be seen as 'Jurassic Management'.

When someone thinks there must be a better way, there usually is. Part of that better way is to have clear business goals and to treat your staff as colleagues who work with you to achieve those goals, rather than for you. Good delegation and good coaching are part of that better way.

The information in this book is based on what I have learned as a manager and a trainer over the last 28 years. Much of that has been learned by watching people do it right and do it wrong, and from my own experiences of getting it right and getting it wrong. If the outcome of this book is that it helps you to get it right more frequently than I have done, then it will have fulfilled its purpose.

I owe a debt of gratitude to all the managers I have learned from in the past and all the staff I have experimented on as well – at times even I did not realize I was experimenting. My thanks also go to the many management trainers and writers who have influenced me over the years. Inevitably they have left their influence on this book. Wherever possible I have tried to acknowledge sources of both information and ideas but sometimes that has not been possible. To my surprise I have found that the origins of some of the ideas I have learned from others and used for years are not readily known, even though the ideas themselves are widely accepted and used. These ideas have achieved the honour of being treated as axiomatic, even though someone must have been the originator. To people who may recognize their own ideas that are not acknowledged I apologize, and I would be delighted to hear from them so that due acknowledgement may be given in any future work.

Many short case studies have been used to illustrate points and they are all based on real events. A few have been modified slightly to strengthen the learning points or to protect identities.

1

The Importance of Delegation and Coaching

One mother recently said that many years ago, when her children were small, she had a nervous breakdown. She had convinced herself that she was the only person in the world who could change a nappy well enough for her babies. Only she could wash and bathe and feed them just right. Her husband could not do these things well enough, nor any of her friends. Only she could bring the necessary love and skill that was needed. The result was that her health suffered drastically and affected the children she was trying to nurture. It is not only managers who are nervous of letting go and delegating. It is not only managers who make themselves ill by failing to do so.

Delegation and coaching have been described as a manager's most difficult tasks. At one end of the scale, like the mother just mentioned, it is so easy to delegate too little in the belief that only you can bring just the right amount of expertise to do the job well enough. At the other extreme it is just as easy to dump tasks on people in the belief that they already know what is expected and have the skills to do it. Neither amounts to good delegation and neither shows one iota of coaching.

Have we not all, at some time in our career, dumped a task on someone for which he or she had neither the knowledge nor the skills to complete it properly? And have we not all, with an iron grip, held onto tasks that someone else could have done perfectly well?

Good delegation and good coaching take care and thought and a confident and generous attitude of mind, but the rewards are great.

If managers are to achieve their own levels of optimum

performance in their jobs then delegation and coaching are not options, they are necessities. Most of us do not delegate and coach anywhere near as well as we could. All it needs is more care and thought, some skills which can be learned, a higher level of trust, and a willingness to take a little more manageable risk.

One would think that, as with most management techniques, since delegation and coaching have been around for a long time they would be widely understood and practised but they are not. Some people seem to delegate and coach naturally. Some have to learn the skills through painful experience and maybe only slowly accept them as essential tools of the trade. Some refuse to accept them at all.

Delegation seems to be practised more widely than coaching, or at least the word is used more often, but too frequently it is done badly. A university student was recently chastised by her boss. She was doing a temporary job during her summer holiday and her manager complained about one task she had done. Having little to lose she replied, 'You did not tell me properly what you wanted me to do and you certainly didn't show me.' It sounds like a fairly typical case of poor delegation and zero coaching, another example of the 'my staff can read my mind' approach to communication. Probably many people have wanted to say something similar to their manager but have feared they had too much to lose if they did.

It is a little like the fable of the three little pigs and the wolf. One pig built his house of straw and was devoured by the hungry wolf. The second built his house of sticks but escaped to live again. The third built his house of bricks and not only survived the wolf's attack but killed the wolf by luring it down the brick chimney and into a roaring fire. Managers who refuse to delegate and coach are eventually devoured by a wolf called over-work. They, not the wolf, get 'burned out'. Others suffer from stress and too much work but eventually find that their staff can rescue them if they are asked to and if they are helped to learn the skills involved. The investment of time needed more than repays the cost. The third type of manager seems to devour work through delegation, stoking the fires within his or her staff by coaching them, so that together they incinerate tasks and problems.

NOT A FAD

Managers can be forgiven for being sceptical about new management fads and trends. Too many fanciful management ideas have been launched down the slipway of publicity only to leave wreckage in their wake. Some contain sound principles but they are dressed up as new theories which have to be stripped away to leave the sound kernel that was always at the heart for those who could find it.

When dealing with the management of people, genuinely new concepts are bound to be rare, very rare. People have been managing people for millennia. Good people-management tools are based on good and trustful relationships and have stood the test of time. Delegation and coaching are such tools.

Consider the following case study as described in one of the oldest books still easily available, the *Book of Exodus* in the *Bible*.

CASE STUDY

About 3,500 years ago Moses led the ancient Israelites out of captivity in Egypt. The book of Exodus recounts a vivid story of delegation and advice, if not actual coaching. After the escape, Moses was the leader of a nation of some '600,000 men, not counting women and children' and was responsible for getting them across a hostile desert to an occupied Promised Land. People brought disputes to him for him to settle and they formed a queue that lasted all day. When his father-in-law, Jethro, visited he thought things could be handled better. 'Why are you doing this all alone, with people standing here from morning to night to consult you?' Jethro asked.

Moses explained that he was judging the disputes. 'When two people have a dispute, they come to me, and I decide which one of them is right...'

Jethro told him, 'You will wear yourself out and these people as well. This is too much for you to do alone. Now let me give you some good advice, and God will be with you.' Jethro pointed out the difference between the very important leadership issues that Moses should deal with personally and the routine administrative and judicial matters that others could do. He suggested a solution that Moses could implement: to select trustworthy men and delegate to them permanently the role of judge with the proviso that they could still bring the most difficult cases to Moses for judgment. Moses took the suggestion and acted on it.

Learning points:

As a case study the story of Moses and Jethro illustrates some essential ingredients of delegation that were obvious to a wise mentor 3,500 years ago.

- ❑ Managers must free themselves from routine tasks so that they can do the leadership things only they can do.
- ❑ Many tasks can be delegated to others if they are helped to learn how to do them and are given the authority to act.
- ❑ People to whom tasks are delegated (delegates) act on behalf of the manager and with the manager's authority.
- ❑ Managers retain overall responsibility and accountability to their own superiors.
- ❑ Routine tasks are accomplished more quickly.
- ❑ The manager must provide extra support for the most difficult problems.
- ❑ A wise coach is a valuable asset.
- ❑ The coach does not make the decision, the learner does.

You cannot do it all

If a great man like Moses could not do it all then neither can you. As Jethro put it, you will wear yourself out if you try. The young mother who suffered a nervous breakdown because of her refusal to accept that others could care for her baby could have taught or coached her husband and friends to do things her way. Better still she could have watched them to see if their way was in fact better than her way. Many people suffer from too much stress. How much of that could be relieved by sensible delegation?

One supervisor at a telephone call centre was a natural worrier. He worried about the hand-over he received from the previous shift and about the hand-over he gave to the following shift. He worried about how his team did their jobs because they had to cover a quarter of the country. What if they got things wrong? Most of his staff were good but he monitored them all very closely because if things did go wrong he would be held accountable by his own manager. In fact things very rarely went wrong. Even if they did, no lives were threatened. He and they did a very competent job but that did not stop him having a nervous breakdown because he was frightened of 'letting go'.

The plain fact is that companies employ many people because they recognize that many people are needed to do all the work. Naturally they want those people to work as near to full capacity as possible for as much of the time as possible. If one person could do it all then there would only be one person, the chief executive. However the chief executive cannot do it all and shares his or her work with some others, the directors. None of them can do it all either so they also share some of their work with senior managers, and so on. The sharing continues so that, eventually, we all get a share of the work. Ideally, the least expensive person who can do a task to the standard needed is the one who does it.

Think of how a warship is crewed. An experienced person is in charge: the captain. The captain delegates specific responsibilities to others: navigation to the navigation officer, weapons to the weapons officer, and so on. Each has a role and each has others to help him or her to achieve it, but overall responsibility still lies with the captain. If the weapons officer decides to shoot up a luxury liner, both he and the captain face a court-martial.

ROLE OF MANAGEMENT

It is usually said that management is about achieving results through other people, that is by delegating work to them. However, today's world changes fast and a company that only looks to today's problems will be out of business tomorrow, so management is now about more than simply achieving results.

Managers today cannot just delegate today's problems, they must also ensure that their staff are ready for tomorrow's challenges. They must develop their staff in a variety of ways and one of the best and least expensive methods of doing that is to coach them in new skills and delegate tasks to them so that they can then use those new skills.

It has not always been so. Traditionally a manager's role has been to plan, organize, motivate and control. Goals have been issued, rules and procedures written and a bureaucracy established to maintain control. Opposing views have been held about workers' attitudes to work. At one extreme is the idea that people dislike

> **Traditional view of management:**
>
> - ❑ Planning
> - ❑ Organizing
> - ❑ Motivating
> - ❑ Controlling

work and that they have to be coerced and will avoid responsibility (this is known as Theory X and is discussed in Chapter 6).

In today's climate, with more liberal management and a better-educated workforce, things can be different even if it is not always so in practice. When people have studied hard and trained hard to achieve their qualifications and positions, they must continue to learn if they want to retain their professionalism. They will not take kindly to being denied opportunities to generate new ideas and learn as they work. Either they learn or they leave.

If managers want to retain professional or ambitious staff, they must develop them. There is no alternative. Theory Y takes hold, proclaiming the view that workers see work as natural, that they gain satisfaction from it under the right conditions and will even seek responsibility. Delegation and coaching encourage that view to become and remain reality.

So coaching and delegation have two distinct business benefits:

1. They enable a small number of senior staff to ensure that the countless jobs that must be done if the organization is to achieve its business aims are achieved, ideally as efficiently and effectively as possible and using the minimum number of people.
2. They help to ensure that the staff are more effective and fulfilled and keep on learning and so are more likely to stay with the company. This retains expertise within the company and reduces recruitment costs.

Modern managers are expected to be leaders, not just managers. John Adair (1979) has wisely expressed the modern role of a manager as having three overlapping core responsibilities: achieving the task, building and maintaining the team, and motivating and developing the individual. This task-team-individual view of the role of management is well known and used in management training. These three responsibilities intertwine and all draw on the various roles taken by people who call themselves managers.

Adair and others also recognize that many managers have a professional role to fulfil as well, perhaps as an accountant, or as an engineer, or as a teacher or whatever. We are drawn into seeing management as a complex process that involves:

- ❑ **Managing** others so that tasks are achieved – through delegation.
- ❑ **Leading** teams and individuals so that changes can be faced and challenges met.
- ❑ **Performing** a professional role, which includes using and developing one's own professional skills.
- ❑ **Developing** individuals (including coaching them) so that they and the company can face the challenges of today and meet those of tomorrow with confidence.

All this is set in a turbulent and sometimes chaotic world where there is either not enough information or there is too much of it, where things change too fast, where best actions are not always clear and best intentions do not always work.

Delegation and coaching are therefore strategic weapons in a

Table 1.1 *A modern view of management (after Adair)*

Responsibilities	Roles
Achieve the tasks	Managing
Build and maintain the team	Leading
Motivate and develop individuals	Developing/Coaching
Achieve own professional tasks	Performing

company's armoury. They are not optional items for managers to play with.

THREE MOTIVES FOR ACTION

You may be able to think of many reasons for embracing the skills of delegation and coaching but basically they fall into three categories – and all three were present 3,500 years ago in Moses's day. We will look at them in detail in the next chapter. They are:

1. To achieve more for the organization.
2. To save time for you.
3. To motivate and develop your people.

These three motives are not just valid at work. They are as valid in the home, in the golf club, at church or at any other place where people come together. The child who helps with the washing up is being developed for later life. Probably the most important delegation and coaching you will ever do will not be at work. It will be at home where by coaching your children and by delegating to them you will help them to grow into tomorrow's useful and responsible citizens.

A natural pairing

It is quite possible to delegate and not to coach. If people already have the knowledge and skills that are required, and have the right attitude to the task and to those involved, then there is no need to coach them when delegating the task to them.

However if they need to learn new knowledge and skills, or if you need to persuade them to modify some behaviour patterns, then coaching and delegation together may be a good way to make progress.

The coaching may follow more formal learning, such as after a training course or a learning package, or it may stand alone. Whenever it occurs, and for whatever reason, when coaching takes place it should always be accompanied by delegation. How else will they learn properly if they are not allowed to do the job? Can you imagine teaching a child to ride a bike without allowing it to get on and ride?

Delegation is not always accompanied by coaching, such as when the individual is already competent.
Coaching should always be accompanied by delegation, to let the person learn by doing the task.

Expressed as a Venn diagram:

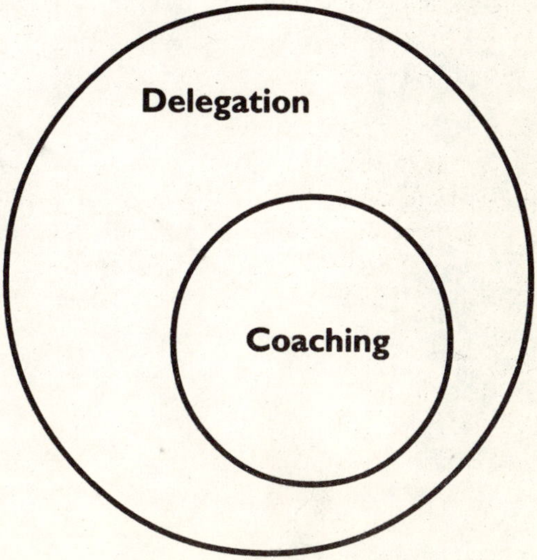

Figure 1.1 *Relationship between delegation and coaching*

Some questions

1. What percentage of your time at work do you devote to coaching your staff right now?
2. What percentage of your time do you think you should devote to coaching your staff?
3. How can you close the gap if there is one?
4. What extra percentage of your tasks could you delegate to your staff?
5. How important do you think your own management believes coaching is, judging by the time you see them devote to it?
6. Does your own manager encourage you to delegate to your staff?
7. Does your own manager encourage you to coach your staff?
8. Who is the best delegator you know and what can you learn from him or her?
9. Who is the best coach you know and what can you learn from him or her?
10. Right now what is your most important task at work that someone else could do?

2

WIN-WIN-WIN

One of our natural human traits is that it is often much easier to persuade ourselves to do something if we can see or suspect some sort of advantage to ourselves. If delegation and coaching are to be truly successful then there must be advantages both to the manager and to the subordinate, and indeed there are. There are also great advantages to the organization as well.

In negotiations people often talk about win-win and win-lose situations. In the win-win situation both parties come away feeling satisfied and happy with the results. Both 'win'. In the win-lose situation one party is disgruntled because they feel they have lost while the other is happy because they 'won'. In reality, when one party feels disgruntled they may take their trade elsewhere next time and so in the long term the 'winner' might actually lose.

In delegation and coaching it is likely that all three parties, the manager, the subordinates and the organization, can come out as winners: a win-win-win situation. Let us take a look at what each has to gain.

BENEFITS FOR THE MANAGER

Time and stress

Are you still at the office after your staff have gone home? Managers who delegate too little inevitably get bogged down in the minutiae of the business and can lose sight of the grand plan. Routine and repetitive work drives out the more innovative and creative work that a manager ought to be doing. When managers are overwhelmed by routine detailed work it is likely to be because they are poor at delegation.

As some wit has observed, time is a non-renewable resource. It is certainly precious. In normal circumstances it is silly for managers to do tasks that more junior members of staff can do to the required standard. One of the main ways in which managers can free up time for themselves, in order to concentrate on management, is by delegating tasks.

Coaching will cost you an investment of time as you help other people to learn but the payback is immense. As you delegate tasks which previously you would have had to do yourself, you start to reap the benefits and you can go on reaping for as long as those staff stay with you. The pressure on you can be reduced and your level of stress with it. You will have more time, perhaps not as much as initially you might have hoped for, but ultimately you will have more time for your own achievements.

Achievements

As Moses found, if you embrace delegation and coaching you will achieve more. You will achieve more yourself because you will have more time to devote to your important management tasks and you will achieve more through your staff. They will accept more responsibility and become more effective through learning to make their own decisions. This gives you a double set of benefits in terms of achievements, your own and those of your staff. 'Give me a lever and I will move the world,' said Archimedes. The purpose of a lever is to amplify force. You apply force at one end of a lever and you can lift an object at the other end that is otherwise too heavy to lift. Stephen Covey has likened management to a lever that moves tasks. By delegating you move the fulcrum or pivot nearer to the subordinate and away from the manager. This creates extra lift and more tasks are achieved than would otherwise be achieved.

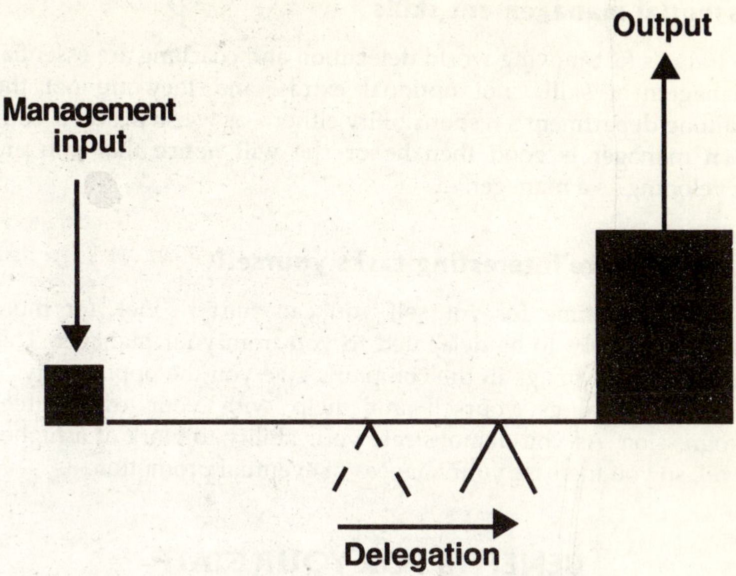

Figure 2.1 *The manager as a lever (after Covey)*

Self-esteem

Not only will you actually achieve more, but you will also increase your sense of achievement and self-esteem through helping others to develop and perhaps go on to better things partly because of your efforts. There is, of course, a cost to you. You have to be willing and able to stand back and see your staff receive praise and reward for things that you used to do yourself, but you should by then have received your own praise and reward as well – if you have a good manager yourself.

> A ceramic tiling specialist was complimented on the work his young apprentice had performed and the cheerful way he had done it. One of the great rewards for him, he said, was to see young people learn and develop and become skilled at the job. This was especially true when they left and started their own little business and he knew he had helped someone to find his or her own place in the world.

Essential management skills

In today's fast-moving world delegation and coaching are essential management skills, not optional extras, and they are not the training department's responsibility either – as we shall see. If your own manager is good then he or she will notice that you are developing as a manager.

Receive more interesting tasks yourself

As you free time for yourself you can start to look for more interesting tasks to be delegated to you from your manager. This can raise your image in the company, give you the opportunity to learn new things yourself and help with your own career progression. As you demonstrate your ability to work at a higher level, so you increase your chances of eventual promotion.

BENEFITS FOR YOUR STAFF

Individuals may be fearful when asked to take on new tasks, especially if they have never done them before, but there are benefits for them also. It is essential that you reassure them that with your help they can do it and that they will have your help as long as they need it. You have confidence in them. They have taken on many new tasks in the past and been successful and they can do it again.

Development

Not everyone feels that they want to be developed, not all the time anyway. Delegation, with or without specific coaching, does develop people. They learn new information and gain new skills. They may find themselves co-operating with people in the business they have not worked with before and they may see aspects of the business that have been hidden from them until now. That may develop a new warmth towards the business and new attitudes to achieving success.

New horizons can be opened to them, although of course not every newly delegated task is so revealing. Some can be mundane. When delegating tasks it is important to ensure that specific individuals receive a mix of new tasks, the interesting as well as the mundane. Never just delegate the dross.

It feels good

If interesting and challenging tasks are delegated then it feels good to the delegate. Any job can become dull after a time of doing the same old things week after week so there is some excitement in being asked to do something new.

There is also the feeling of being respected and valued and trusted which raises self-esteem. One of the best rewards a manager can give to an employee is thanks and praise. Unfortunately, in our society, it is something that many managers feel embarrassed to do. A few words of thanks and praise for a job well done as an introduction to a briefing on a new task demonstrate that an employee is valued. It all adds to job satisfaction.

Jobs are enriched

As managers learn to delegate more of the interesting and challenging tasks they have previously kept to themselves so other people's jobs are enriched and become more interesting. It is not just at work where this happens. Think of teenagers who have just learned to drive and how helpful they suddenly become at running chores such as picking up their little sister from her music class.

They use their initiative

When given more responsibility and a degree of authority people start to use their own initiative and imagination more. Drawing on their personal strengths they can propose new ideas and solutions. Of course this has to be monitored, quite closely at first until you have confidence in their judgement, but isn't this what you want to happen?

BENEFITS FOR THE COMPANY

Cost efficient

Organizations operate most efficiently when all the important tasks not only get done, and done on time, but also are done at the least cost. If managers do tasks that could be done to the required standard by their staff then not only is time wasted but also costs are unnecessarily high. If there is a magic answer to the question of how to increase productivity and reduce costs then delegation and coaching are part of it.

One of the silliest fads of recent times has been the management concentration on head count instead of on staff costs. In many companies inexpensive junior staff have been made redundant, leaving expensive managers doing essential but routine tasks which ought to be delegated to others.

Teams become more flexible

Use delegation to move tasks around a team, so widening the skill base and increasing flexibility. Not only does this help to motivate people but it builds in a degree of contingency planning for when problems arise such as a major sickness of an employee.

Teamwork developed

As tasks are delegated people come into contact with others whom they have not worked closely with before. This helps to foster teamwork, maybe just within your own work group or on a larger scale within the company. It is not only you as the manager who can coach – use your staff to coach one another as well.

Workloads are balanced

A problem in some teams is that some people have more to do than others. Effective delegation can ensure an equitable balance of work and that all tasks get done.

Keep good staff, develop poorer staff

Recruiting staff, especially professional staff, is a very expensive and time-consuming process. Job advertisements in national newspapers can cost tens of thousands of pounds, and that is only one part of the full cost. When high-quality people are bored they look for pastures new. Good delegation prevents boredom and helps to keep good staff within the team, or at least within the company. Less competent staff can be developed into more useful members of the team through careful coaching and delegation.

A more powerful workforce

The workforce can be developed as a whole through an organization-wide policy of coaching and delegation. The organization itself can climb the value chain, gradually moving into more profitable business areas on the back of a more skilled workforce. Yet many companies inadvertently demotivate their staff by ignoring their talents.

Aids communication

An essential step in the delegation process is to ensure that members of staff understand why they are being asked to do new tasks. Explaining why gives managers the chance to relate these tasks to their own objectives and ultimately to the company's objectives, so helping more staff to understand more of the business plans.

Geographical dispersal

As an organization expands and opens branches in new towns, cities and countries, responsibility and authority have to be delegated from the centre. The same principle holds for a department that expands from one building to another, from one floor to another, or from one office to two.

Customer service

Things go wrong in all organizations, however good they are. When something goes wrong it is impossible to give good customer service if employees are not empowered to act without consulting 'the boss'. It is not good customer service to keep a disgruntled customer waiting while someone checks with head office to see if they can exchange faulty goods. With certain safeguards in place, the power to act must be delegated to those who serve where the action takes place.

DISADVANTAGES

If it is all so wonderful how can there be any disadvantages? Often the disadvantages are more perceived than real, but wrong perceptions seem real and therefore they are important. If someone wrongly believes that there is a disadvantage the effect is much the same as if they were right.

Managers lose tasks they enjoy

It is a fact of life that as we are promoted we tend to hold onto tasks that we enjoyed doing in the old job. It is a fact but it is a mistake. We have to learn to let go. We also need to let go of some things we enjoy doing in our present job so that we can delegate them to others, for now there are even more interesting and exciting things for us to do. Learn to take pleasure from seeing others succeed under your coaching. Let go of the old so that you can take hold of the new.

Staff are not capable or experienced

How do you know they are not capable? They may not yet be skilled or experienced but they may be capable of things you have not dreamed of. There are many stories of minnows at work who were giants outside. Learn to see people as potentially capable even though they are not yet skilled or experienced. That opens opportunities for you to develop their professional skills and your coaching skills. Of course you are not going to attempt the impossible. The people you coach must have the potential to achieve the delegated tasks. The question is: Do you fail to see their potential?

As for experience, how else will they gain experience if they are not allowed to try? Through briefings, coaching, monitoring and feedback you use your own experience to balance their lack. As their experience and confidence builds so your monitoring might be reduced.

Risk of losing control

It is true that some managers do lose control once they delegate. It depends on what you mean by control. If you delegate well, using the process described later, you will relinquish some control while retaining management of the overall project. You will set the goals and targets but manage their achievement through monitoring and feedback. You will no longer put in the stitches but you will still design and produce the tapestry.

It takes too much time

It does take time. You need to devote considerable time to begin with to briefing, discussing, coaching, monitoring and getting feedback from the individual and from others, but this is an investment. You may indeed be able to do it quicker yourself right now, but where does that place you in a month's time, or a year's time? It puts you just where you are now, no further forward. If you do not invest time now, you will not gain the reward.

Depending on the task in question there can be an immediate gain in time, not a loss. With good coaching and delegation a junior member of staff can almost immediately do the time-consuming jobs of running around, gathering information, sorting out facts and so on while you do other things. This gives an immediate saving of your time, not a loss.

They don't have time

It ought to be true that your staff are fully occupied right now but that does not mean that they cannot take delegated tasks. It is a question of priorities. No busy team of people can do all the tasks that come their way, inevitably some tasks do not get done. That is right and proper, provided that the abandoned tasks are the least important ones and are not essential. In most work situations there are many low-importance tasks just waiting for the chop. Get rid of them and so make time for more important delegated tasks. You may also find that you can reallocate tasks from one subordinate to another to create time for a newly delegated task.

If your organization has suffered from the head count malaise now might be the time to argue for a new junior member of staff to join you. Be sure you can cover the costs from the increased revenue that will be generated by more effective working.

Manager's job will be diminished

Some managers may fear that their jobs will become less interesting if they delegate too many tasks to subordinates. Others fear that they will then have too little to do and so be made redundant, or that their manager may think that if their tasks can be delegated down then their job was rated at too high a level and should be downgraded.

A climate of fear in a company is a terrible thing and does nothing to encourage good practice, including delegation. The simple answer is that productivity will increase and this should be provable. Further, in time, you should be able to volunteer to take some more interesting tasks off your own manager so relieving his or her pressure.

Achieving results through others and seeing them develop their skills and career under your care are very satisfying achievements. Remember what the ceramic tiler said in the case study on p.23. Skilful coaching and delegation open up new avenues to you as a manager and these avenues bring their own rewards. Your job will not be diminished, it will be enhanced.

Staff may be fearful

Staff may feel that they are not up to it or that things will go wrong. Reassure them that you will be alongside them. There will be stages within delegated tasks beyond which they cannot go until you are satisfied or have given further help and coaching. They must have confidence that you will still support them if things do go wrong. The blame culture is not going to be introduced. Their feedback and your monitoring should be good enough to correct mistakes well before they cause serious problems. It is like helping a timid person to cross a boulder-strewn torrent. You take it together. You will be there when you are needed.

Manager may be fearful

Managers can live in fear of all sorts of things, one being that their staff may actually do the job better than they can do it themselves. Overcoming this fear is called maturity. It is one of the joys of management that some of your staff can do things better than you can. It is one of the duties of management that you make maximum use of their expertise. Maybe one of your staff is destined to be a future chief executive. Is that any reason for you to try to hold him or her back? Take pride in the fact that some of his or her skills have been learned from you.

If management is about achieving tasks through other people then you will want good people to work for you. Of course they will do some things better than you. The fact that you can manage such people and get the best from them is a positive reflection on you, not a negative one. Enjoy the feeling.

If you fear that they will make a mess of things and you will get the blame then use the process described later to ensure that safety nets and stoppage points are in place so that your monitoring and control will detect errors before they become important. You can minimize any risks and, together, you can get things back on the right path.

Passing the buck

If your staff feel that by delegating you are passing the buck, or that they will be doing your job for you, then it is time to explain the facts of modern corporate life to them.

More has to be achieved by fewer people. Inevitably this means that tasks are delegated down.

For cost-efficiency reasons all tasks have to be done at the least expensive level. The competition are doing it, so if you do not do it you will not be competitive. If you are not competitive then you could all be looking for new jobs.

This will make their jobs more interesting and perhaps more exciting. They will learn new skills that will help them to build their careers. If they are beyond the career-building stage of life then just recognize that the pace of change affects everyone today. No one's job stays the same for long nowadays.

Staff want more pay

If extra pay, perhaps a small bonus, is possible then explain what is needed for it to happen, but base the award on results not just on effort. Set their expectations that a modest bonus is possible but that it has to be earned. If it is not going to be considered, say so from the start – if they ask.

SUMMARY:
ADVANTAGES AND DISADVANTAGES

The advantages and disadvantages discussed above are listed below, together with a few more that might apply to you.

Advantages

- ❑ Achieves results.
- ❑ Raises your self-esteem and gives a sense of achievement.
- ❑ They feel good, raises their self-esteem.
- ❑ Saves you time, releases you for more important jobs, time to think.

- ❑ Reduces your workload.
- ❑ Demonstrates essential management skills.
- ❑ Helps you to cope with the pace of change.
- ❑ Boosts own position, receive more interesting tasks from your manager.
- ❑ Develops you and your staff.
- ❑ Jobs are enriched.
- ❑ Staff use their initiative.
- ❑ It is cost effective.
- ❑ Builds better and more flexible teams.
- ❑ Workloads are balanced.
- ❑ Keeps good staff, develops poorer ones.
- ❑ Aids communications.
- ❑ Raises morale.
- ❑ Provides cover in your absence.
- ❑ Decisions are made closer to the action.
- ❑ Tests promotion potential of staff.
- ❑ Yields evidence for performance appraisals.

Disadvantages

More perceived than real:

- ❑ Own job may be diminished.
- ❑ No longer do some things you enjoy doing.
- ❑ Risk losing control, they'll know more than you.
- ❑ Staff not capable.
- ❑ Staff not experienced.
- ❑ Quicker and better to do it yourself.
- ❑ Staff may be fearful.
- ❑ You may be fearful. Risky, what if they fail?
- ❑ You may be fearful, must be seen to be busy.
- ❑ It's passing the buck.
- ❑ They will object, other colleagues or the union will object.
- ❑ They may want more money.

DEFINITIONS

There are usually potential problems when we try to define the meaning of words used in inter-personal relationships. You may disagree with my definition and I with yours, although that may not matter very much. The problem is more likely to be that neither definition will cover all eventualities. Real situations tend to be fuzzier than definitions would have us believe.

If we try to find a definition that covers all situations we end up with something that is too long to be useful let alone memorable. It is better to have something short and sweet that expresses the gist of the concept and can be remembered, rather than something long and legalistic.

Delegation

The *Concise Oxford Dictionary* defines the verb to delegate as to 'commit (authority, power, etc) to an agent or deputy, entrust (a task) to another person, send or authorize (a person) as a representative'. That gives us the broad outline of delegation but more is needed if we are to use the definition to help us to improve our delegation skills.

Delegation also involves a responsibility to others, usually to your own manager or customer, plus a responsibility to the subordinate to whom you delegate the task. You retain your overall responsibility to your manager or customer, not for actually doing the task but for ensuring that it is done to the standard required. This is sometimes called accountability instead of responsibility. To your delegate you have a responsibility to ensure that there is a clear understanding between the two of you, that you let him or her get on with the job and that by monitoring performance you will prevent any disasters. This leads us to the following definition of delegation:

Delegation is entrusting authority and responsibility to another to complete a clearly defined and agreed task under your supervision, while retaining your overall responsibility for the success of the work.

This highlights that the responsibility for achievement is shared between the manager and the delegate, and that the subordinate is just as accountable to the manager as the manager is to his or her own boss.

The sharing concept is important. A delegated task is not given to a subordinate so that the manager can then forget about it, or it should not be. That is dumping and dumped tasks often return to haunt you. Delegating is not just telling other people to do something and sitting back while they do it. It involves giving staff the resources and the responsibility to use their own initiative so that the agreed objectives can be achieved, and accepting your own responsibility for the success. Saying, 'Here is a job, get on with it,' is not delegation, it is abdication.

Coaching

There can be similar problems when we try to define what is meant by coaching. The dictionary describes a coach as 'a private tutor' which is an excellent starting point. It also describes coaching as training, giving hints to, and priming with facts. This can be misleading. Coaching and training are not the same thing and coaching is certainly not about priming with facts, not in the modern business sense anyway.

Coaching is not simply about showing people, or telling them, how to do something. If you only do that there is no guarantee that any learning will take place. Coaching is far more than that. Coaching puts the emphasis on helping the learner to learn, rather than on getting the teacher to teach. It involves guiding and encouraging people to achieve results by helping them to learn for themselves while doing the job. Real work is the vehicle for learning. Its ultimate target is to help individuals to release their own potential and improve their performance.

Coaching is the provision of guidance and encouragement to help people to learn for themselves by doing the job.

This definition contains the essential elements that differentiate coaching from other forms of learning, especially training. Coaching is about helping the person to learn a new skill or behaviour by doing the job and achieving the desired results. It is the real thing and the genuine result is required just as if the manager was actually doing the task.

That is why it goes hand in hand with delegation. Delegate tasks to people who as yet do not know how to do them and coach them through the work. At the end you will have tasks completed to the standards required and staff who can do them next time with far less assistance, if any at all. A double benefit to you as a manager.

In summary: Delegation is about what to do, coaching is about learning while doing it.

PERSONAL QUALITIES NEEDED

To delegate and coach successfully certain personal qualities and competencies or skills are needed by the manager. The personal qualities include:

- ❑ A caring attitude towards your staff.
- ❑ A willingness to listen to them.
- ❑ An inquisitive nature that wants to know what they have done, and how and why they did it.
- ❑ The will to trust others and demonstrate that trust to them.
- ❑ The ability to 'let go'.

The competencies or skills needed are mainly interpersonal skills such as:

- ❑ Questioning techniques.
- ❑ The ability to listen attentively and accurately.
- ❑ Being able to explain things clearly.
- ❑ Knowing how and when to monitor performance.
- ❑ The ability to give fair and sensitive feedback and elicit it from others.
- ❑ Being an accurate and perceptive observer.
- ❑ Making judgements that are fair.
- ❑ Showing respect for others and gaining their respect in return.

For some managers it is the personal qualities that pose the biggest problem, especially letting go and trusting. These problems are based on the fear of failure, a fear that can be overcome by using a good process, as described in the next two chapters.

3

DELEGATION

Earlier we defined delegation as:

> *Entrusting authority and responsibility to another to complete a clearly defined and agreed task under your supervision, while retaining your overall responsibility for the success of the work.*

In this and the next chapter we will look at how people often fall short of achieving that in practice and what can be done to improve and get nearer to the ideal.

For most managers delegation is about sharing tasks with individuals, usually subordinates, but it can be broader than that. For example, it is possible to delegate to groups of people or teams, or even to another organization. That is how major projects are achieved. It is often the case that one company manages the project while others do the work and that is a form of delegation, usually agreed through a contract. Military manoeuvres and joint business ventures also require a sharing between organizations. You can also delegate upwards to your own manager or sideways to a colleague. It can be more difficult than downward delegation but sometimes it is more appropriate for your manager or another colleague to do a task for you than for you to do it yourself. Such occasions can arise when there is an emergency, or time is very short, or their particular knowledge or skills are needed. We are going to concentrate on delegation to subordinates but the principles apply to the other forms of delegation.

DELEGATION IN PRACTICE

Even if you are willing to delegate it can be a problem deciding what parts of your job to delegate to whom and when and what support they will need, and then have the patience and courage to see it through. This is especially true if they make a few mistakes and you get some criticism from your boss or internal customers. It is even worse if an external customer suffers.

Think about a few questions to see how well you delegate now. These are typical of those posed on delegation training courses.

Self-analysis questions

1. Are you frightened to let go?
2. Do you take work home most evenings?
3. Are you the last to leave most evenings?
4. Do you do a lot of routine or repetitive work?
5. Do you often do things that your staff could do?
6. Do you hold onto some tasks just because you enjoy them?
7. Do your people frequently interrupt you for information?
8. Are you frustrated because there are too many unfinished jobs around?
9. Are deadlines usually missed?
10. Is there no time for long-term planning?
11. Is there no time to talk with your staff about their progress?
12. Do you ignore the potential of your staff to generate ideas and suggestions?
13. Are you reluctant to let your staff do parts of your job for you?
14. Do you think that standards will fall if you do not do most things yourself?
15. Do you watch your staff very closely to prevent mistakes?
16. Are you a natural worrier?
17. Do you have disputes because your staff do not understand what you want?
18. Do you criticize more than you praise?
19. Are you fully using your staff's expertise?
20. If you cannot do something today do you look for someone who can?

Do your answers suggest that there is much you can do to improve your delegation?

Are you a manager who drives a smoothly functioning team from the centre like the conductor of an orchestra? Or are you more like a one-man band with sticks and clappers fastened to both hands and feet, and a mouth organ clamped in front of your face, while others mill around trying not to get in the way?

Is your team like an international football team where each player knows his role but moves individually to support others and to open up new opportunities? Or is yours like a team of little boys, where everyone chases the ball to every corner of the pitch, including the captain who is too engrossed to notice?

Good delegation requires you to tread a careful path between what have been called under-delegation and dumping. It is not always easy. The following points illustrate what is needed and what to avoid.

Good delegation requires you to:

- ❑ Decide what you can delegate and what you cannot.
- ❑ Decide who to delegate to, both for staff development and for efficiency.
- ❑ Agree the task in sufficient detail for the individual to understand clearly what is needed and to what standard.
- ❑ Agree the deadline, so that there is no misunderstanding.
- ❑ Use the definitions of the task, standard and deadline as the measures by which both of you can realistically judge success.
- ❑ Let go of whole tasks, not just bits of tasks.
- ❑ Agree the limits, how far they can go without further approval.
- ❑ Agree the resources of people, money, equipment and time.
- ❑ Agree that other jobs have to continue meanwhile, or that some can be put aside or delegated elsewhere.
- ❑ Agree the level of authority you are delegating.
- ❑ Agree what help in terms of training or coaching will be needed and how it will be accomplished.
- ❑ Agree the monitoring and feedback needed, and when and how it will take place.

- ❑ Agree who else needs to be told and who will do the telling and when.
- ❑ Agree that the individuals carry the responsibility and are accountable to you for their actions.
- ❑ Agree that you are accountable to your own boss, that ultimately you carry the can but they get most of the praise.
- ❑ Agree that you will support their decisions, provided they keep within your agreement with them.
- ❑ Show your trust and confidence provided they operate within specified boundaries.

This seems like a daunting list but it need not be, as we shall see later.

Under-delegation

Do you under-delegate? Under-delegation is something to avoid, it involves failing to let go enough. It means:

- ❑ Delegating only menial or trivial tasks.
- ❑ Watching every move your subordinate makes.
- ❑ Hanging on to the things you personally enjoy and are good at, or that get noticed by others.
- ❑ Not developing your staff.
- ❑ Not trusting staff or giving them room to contribute.
- ❑ Missing deadlines.
- ❑ An uneven workload among staff.
- ❑ Being overloaded yourself.
- ❑ Enduring more stress than is necessary.
- ❑ Limiting your own development.
- ❑ Limiting your own promotion prospects by denying yourself opportunities to receive more delegation from above.
- ❑ Frustrating staff and risking losing them.

A small company employed six engineers, four technicians and two skilled handymen. With a full order book the six engineers were permanently busy, worked unpaid overtime and took work home. Each technician reported to one of the engineers and helped only that individual, apart from very occasionally helping another technician. Their workload fluctuated and there were nearly always one or two of them reading the newspaper, or tidying the workbenches and waiting for home time. The handymen attended courses to learn a variety of technical skills but were grossly under utilized. They became good gardeners, even growing prize-winning vegetables in the company grounds.

Dumping

Do you dump things on people rather than delegate? Dumping means:

- ❑ Not agreeing clear goals, targets, feedback and deadlines.
- ❑ Abdicating your own responsibility.
- ❑ Surrendering your controlling influence.
- ❑ Inadequate or non-existent monitoring.
- ❑ Ignoring current workloads and deadlines.
- ❑ Not listening to your staff.
- ❑ Not thinking through to the consequences.
- ❑ Courting disaster and getting nasty surprises.
- ❑ Frustrating staff and risking losing them.
- ❑ Overly authoritarian leadership.
- ❑ Manager thinking things are fine when they definitely are not.
- ❑ Staff moan about being treated like mushrooms; being neglected and kept in the dark. Poor communication.

Being treated like mushrooms

Growers keep mushrooms in the dark and cover them with manure. That is how it feels when you are dumped on – there is poor communication, too much work, you get blamed when it goes wrong and you feel neglected. Do you treat your staff like mushrooms?

A senior salesman told a project engineer that a customer was due to visit in ten minutes but he would not have time to see him. Would the engineer see him instead? The engineer knew little about the case, nothing about the customer, did not work for the salesman, was not being briefed properly, and felt he was being dumped upon. Why, he asked, could the salesman not see him? Because he had a staff meeting, was the reply. The engineer suggested that the salesman should skip the staff meeting and meet his own customer. Ten minutes later the engineer's telephone rang and the receptionist informed him that his visitor had arrived. The visitor was kept waiting while the salesman was dragged from his meeting to face a by now irate customer whom he had tried to avoid.

Excuses

People are wonderful at making up excuses to cover their own lapses. Have you ever used these excuses?

Under-delegation

- ❑ It's easier or quicker to do it myself.
- ❑ If you want a job doing properly, do it yourself.
- ❑ We can't afford a mistake on this one.
- ❑ It's a rush job, no time to teach anyone else.
- ❑ They fouled up last time, I can't trust them this time.
- ❑ I've tried delegation, it didn't work.
- ❑ The customer expects me to be there.
- ❑ My people are overloaded as it is.

Dumping

- ❑ I had to learn the hard way, so can they.
- ❑ You learn better and faster if you just get on with it.
- ❑ It gives them a chance to use their initiative.
- ❑ If I have to explain everything I might as well do it myself in the first place.
- ❑ Let's see what they can do.
- ❑ It sorts out the men from the boys.

When did you last say or think one of these excuses or something similar? Think back over the incident and think clearly about the task and people involved and especially about what you did, said and felt. Replay the whole thing in your mind and decide at what point you could have done things differently so as to achieve better delegation. Next time you catch yourself saying or thinking an excuse – stop and think.

LEVELS OF DELEGATION

Not every delegated task devolves the same level of authority to the junior partner. For example, if you take your children into a self-service café you may:

- ❑ Select something for them.
- ❑ Let them choose between two items.
- ❑ Invite them to suggest what they would like.
- ❑ Invite them to say what they would like and then let them get it.
- ❑ Let them go and get what they want without telling you.
- ❑ Let them get what they want and tell them what to get for you as well.
- ❑ Let them get what they want and ask them to select and bring something for you too.

The level of authority you devolve may depend on several factors. These may include the age of the children, how much you want to spend, whether this is a main meal or a snack, how extravagant they are, whether it is a special occasion such as a birthday, what mood you are in, and so on.

At work the level of authority you delegate will depend on factors equivalent to these, including what mood you are in. Obviously the effect your mood has on your delegation should be minimal if you are to achieve consistency.

At one extreme subordinates may simply be asked to gather information, check facts, pass on a message, or other straightforward tasks. At the other extreme they may be given full control with virtually no feedback needed other than, perhaps, to say it is finished.

Which level you operate at will usually depend on three main considerations, a sort of You/Them/It:

You: Your comfort level.
Them: The individual.
It: The task.

The range of levels at which you can delegate are not as fixed as they might seem but form a continuous spectrum from the simplest level to the most complex. For the sake of illustrating the range we can say there are six levels, although you could easily argue for more or less.

Level 1: Look into it. Gather the information.
Level 2: As level 1 but suggest alternative courses of action, with pros and cons.
Level 3: As level 2 but make a recommendation.
Level 4: As level 3 but start after I agree. Proceed to Point X and seek further approval.
Level 5: This is the problem. Start when you are ready and tell me soon afterwards. Proceed to Point X then check with me.
Level 6: This is the problem. Solve it and tell me when it is finished. Let me know if you need my help.

Table 3.1 illustrates this as an ascending granting of authority.

Table 3.1 *Levels of delegation*

Level	Information	Suggestion	Recommendation	Act after approval	Act without approval
1	✔				
2	✔	✔			
3	✔	✔	✔		
4	✔	✔	✔	✔	
5	✔	✔	✔		✔*
6	✔	✔	✔		✔

*with safeguards

Of course, you can imagine other levels but these are representative of what happens in practice. Levels five and six are what some people refer to as empowerment, that is, the power to act within certain limits without further authorization.

As a manager you may instinctively feel very wary of levels five and six yet you probably use them very frequently for trivial tasks, such as photocopying, without any thought. Just think of the huge number of things your staff are allowed to do without asking your permission. You already delegate at levels five and six. The challenge now is to be comfortable when delegating important tasks at these high levels.

Look back at the admittedly arbitrary six levels of delegation and decide at what level most of your delegation occurs. What dissuades you from delegating at higher levels? What can you do about it? The rest of the book should help you to raise the level at which you typically delegate.

Keeping this concept of levels of delegation in mind is very helpful. It keeps you on the right track by preventing you from dumping tasks onto subordinates and it guides you as to what to expect your subordinates to do.

Level 1: A secretary was asked to telephone various suppliers and collect leaflets and quotations for a new photocopier, put them in a file and give them to the manager.

Level 3: A customer was accidentally overcharged by £10 when buying new tyres for his car. After paying by credit card the customer spotted the mistake and asked the mechanic who had processed the payment to correct it. The mechanic apologized, said he was not allowed to make a refund but would send the details to his head office. They would send a cheque within two weeks.

Level 6: A customer was checking out of a large hotel and complained that noisy water pipes in her room had disturbed her sleep. The receptionist apologized, noted the details and took 10 per cent off the bill as an apology.

For many tasks it can be much simpler to think in terms of just three levels of delegation instead of six. These can follow after you have discussed possible courses of action:

Level 1: Approval First: One step at a time. Approval needed for each step.
Level 2: Act and Report: Take action but report back daily, weekly, etc.
Level 3: Full Authority: Act on my behalf. Tell me when it is finished.

WHAT TO DELEGATE

What you delegate is pretty much up to you but some things lend themselves to delegation and others do not.

It is most likely that you will delegate tasks but you can also delegate roles (on-going functions) from within your own post. For example, a manager will often have a budget and will be held responsible for it but it would be quite feasible to delegate the accountancy side of managing the budget to someone else. That person could start by running a system to track how much of the annual budget has been spent, providing the manager with weekly or monthly statements, something like a bank statement. Later your delegate could progress to making predictions and eventually to constructing the budget bid for next year.

Other roles that might be suitable for delegation could include any that require repetitive detailed work, such as routine correspondence, inventory management, health and safety monitoring, and so on. Always there is the proviso that the individual has been appropriately trained or coached and is able to deliver the results to the necessary standard.

Everything you have to deal with, whether role or task, can be pictured along scales of both importance and urgency. As a manager you should be achieving the immediate tasks through other people while you concentrate on the longer-term and more important tasks. Of course life is not always that simple and you will find yourself doing some important, urgent tasks as well. However, the principle is clear: the important and longer-term issues, such as strategic thinking, planning, and so on, are your tasks. You cannot do them if you spend all your time on urgent day-to-day issues that you should have delegated to your staff. You should concentrate on the important and non-urgent issues as much as you possibly can.

So what sort of tasks are ripe for delegation? Most senior managers would expect you to delegate tasks that are:

- ❑ Routine.
- ❑ Complete in themselves.
- ❑ Time-consuming but necessary.
- ❑ Recurring frequently.
- ❑ Ones your subordinates can do better than you.
- ❑ Ones your subordinates can do more economically than you.
- ❑ Regular, such as deputizing for you at routine meetings.
- ❑ Favourites that you tend to keep for yourself, but should not.
- ❑ Pet hates that someone else might enjoy.
- ❑ Large projects or tasks that can be broken down into separate activities, especially if there are tight deadlines.
- ❑ Ones that will add variety to someone else's role.
- ❑ Moving from planning and decision-making to implementation.

WHAT NOT TO DELEGATE

There are some tasks for which there is wide agreement that you really ought not to delegate because of their very nature, things that are yours by the very fact that you are the manager:

- ❑ Company briefings, except if timing is important and you cannot be there.
- ❑ Genuine crises which will need your authority to sort out quickly.
- ❑ Tasks with ill-defined requirements where others could waste a lot of time, unless you have great confidence in them.
- ❑ Unpleasant tasks that you must face up to, such as staff disciplinary measures.
- ❑ Tasks clearly beyond the individuals' ability to perform, even if you coach them.

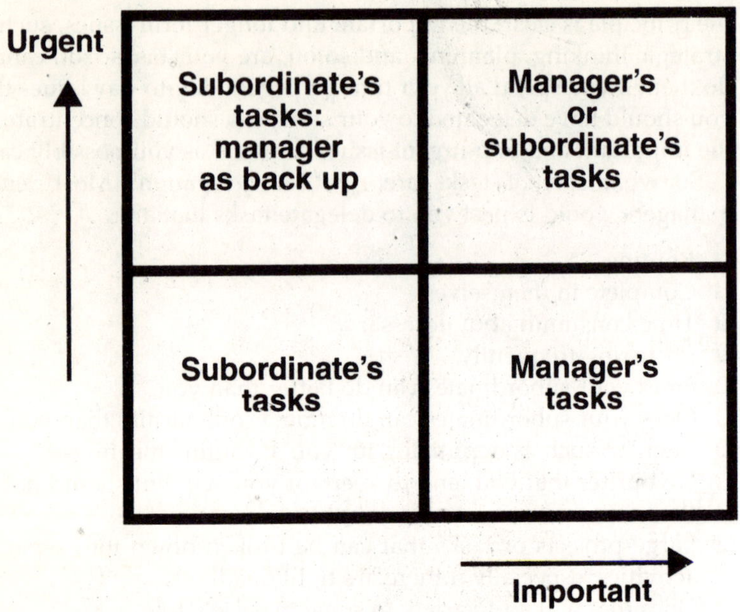

Figure 3.1 *What to delegate*

- ❑ Things the company defines as being your personal responsibility – performance appraisals may be an example.
- ❑ Confidential matters or where special sensitivity is needed, or tasks that the individual has the right to expect the manager to do. The latter could include long-service awards, special recognition, redundancy or termination of employment.
- ❑ Praise for a job well done.
- ❑ Strategy and policy issues.
- ❑ Something vital that only you can do confidently in the time available.
- ❑ Where the individual strongly resists taking on the delegated task. (You should investigate carefully to discover the root cause.)

Also there are some traditional management areas that no manager should delegate, but too many often do by default:

- ❑ Setting your departmental goals.
- ❑ Walking the talk to your staff.
- ❑ Building and protecting your team.
- ❑ Taking the flak for your team.
- ❑ Monitoring your team's results and planning continuous improvement.
- ❑ Planning the development of your team.

CONCLUSION

Think about either the three or six levels of delegation and where you normally operate. What can you do to move to higher levels of delegation? Think about the dangers of both dumping and under-delegation. Run through the checklists again to see if you really do avoid both examples of poor practice. Question your own performance against the lists of things to delegate and not to delegate and try to spot areas where you could improve. Are there tasks that you currently delegate that you ought not to? Are there any that you do yourself that could be handled by others? What are they?

4

A Process for Delegation

Delegation always involves taking a risk, but you take risks every day. Travelling to work involves risk. Almost all business decisions involve taking risks so the fact that there are risks involved in delegating need not worry you. You are used to risks and you know how to deal with them – you minimize them.

A PARENT'S TALE

One day two ageing parents decided to let their mentally-handicapped adult daughter travel on her own by public transport to the day centre she attended. They had long avoided just this situation because of the risks involved, real and imagined. Social services cuts meant there was no longer a private mini-bus available as transport and they realized that before much longer they would not be able to make the journey themselves there and back twice a day to take and collect her. In their hearts they knew they would not be around much longer at all.

Together with their social services care worker they made their plans. First they explained why, soon, she would have to make the journey to and from 'work' alone. She was excited at the prospect. Next they travelled the route with her day after day at the right times, walking across the town centre to the bus station, getting the right bus, 'paying' the fare with a bus pass, changing buses at the right place, disembarking at the right place, and checking her into the day centre on arrival.

After a week she made the journey alone, fully aware that she was being observed every inch of the way. She was praised for getting it right and felt proud of herself. This continued for a while without mishap. Finally she made the journey alone and without being observed at which point she was praised considerably. Soon she was totally accustomed to her new routine but still monitored by her arrival time at her destinations – the centre in the morning and her home in the evening.

Before long she started to stop off in town on her way home to do some window shopping, bringing home news of shops that had opened and others that had closed. Her parent's weekly burden of heavy grocery shopping was alleviated when she started to visit the supermarket each evening and bring home a few things each day.

She was soon on first name terms with a few of the checkout girls who then started to help her to find things she could not locate. Her parents found the girls and thanked them. They offered to read a shopping list if it would help. It did and the weekly burden of grocery shopping for two eighty-year-olds was fully solved.

Learning points:

This true story contains many of the elements of good delegation:

- ❑ There was a problem that had to be solved.
- ❑ The 'managers' were anxious about the risks involved and the ability of the individual. So the risks were identified and planned for.
- ❑ The situation was explained to the person and agreement gained.
- ❑ The requirements of the delegated task were explained and understood. (Get to work safely at the right time and get home safely at the right time.)
- ❑ The responsibilities were agreed (between the parents, the girl and the care worker).
- ❑ The necessary resources were made available (a bus pass).
- ❑ Coaching was given.
- ❑ Others who needed to know were told (the day centre staff).
- ❑ Progress was appropriately monitored, more closely at the beginning than later when progress was smooth.

- ❑ **Progress was rewarded with praise.**
- ❑ **A new situation was achieved where the delegated task was treated as the norm.**
- ❑ **There was an unexpected bonus as a further task was voluntarily taken on.**

This story illustrates several key points about delegation. Before they begin delegates must know as clearly as possible what they are expected to do, how well and by when. With this information they ought to be able to judge success for themselves just as clearly as the manager can and by the same criteria. Identifiable risks must be minimized and planned for. While the task is being performed the manager should monitor performance and include stoppage points, if necessary, beyond which the delegate is not authorized to proceed until certain criteria have been met. These act as safety nets for all involved and prevent disasters if things do go wrong. Delegates should be praised when things go well. If things do go wrong then remember that you as the manager had overall control so it was ultimately your responsibility. Afterwards investigate and learn from any mistakes so that they are not repeated.

Delegation is a three-stage process involving elements before, during and after the task, and each stage has several issues for you to think about and act upon. Let us look at each stage.

BEFORE

An *aide-mémoire* for many managerial situations is provided by the opening stanza of the well-known poem by Rudyard Kipling, *Six Honest Serving Men*. 'I keep six honest serving-men, they taught me all I knew. Their names are What and Why and When, and How and Where and Who.' Personally I abbreviate these to the Six Ws (Yes, I know, but how ends with a W): What, Why, When, How, Where, Who.

Try these six Ws. What has to be done? Who will do it? Why is it needed and why are you delegating it? Who has what responsibility? When has it to be completed by? Where will the delegate get any resources needed? How will you monitor the task? But, note, not how will the delegate do it?

The obvious first things to decide are the task and the person. Which you decide first will depend on your motive. If you are aiming to develop a specific person then the person and his or her development needs come first and you will have to find a task suitable for that development plan. If you have a task that needs doing then the task comes first and you will be looking for someone to do it.

The task

Define the task in terms of what outcomes you want and when you want them. Be specific because there must be clear understanding between you as these criteria will be used by both of you to judge success at the end. The techniques for achieving this are discussed in Chapter 9 and include agreeing objectives, interview skills and negotiating.

- ❑ *Result*: Define the result you want to achieve in terms as precise as necessary for both of you to make a clear judgement at the end. This is sometimes called an objective or outcome. The precision of the definition must be such that the two of you, and any third party involved, clearly understand what is meant. It need go no further than that except that you must ensure that their understanding matches your own. The fact that someone uninvolved in the task may not understand is irrelevant.
- ❑ *Deadline*: Give a specific date, not 'in a month or so'.
- ❑ *Resources*: Now is the time to identify any resources needed and plan for them to be available. Consider: materials, budget, machinery, and access to information, people and IT.
- ❑ *Why*: Be sure you know why this task or role needs to be done and can explain why. Whenever possible describe the link to the departmental or company business plan or objectives. Also have an answer ready for the question, 'Why me?' Is it to develop the individual, provide greater variety of work, increase effectiveness, allow you to do other things, or what?

MEMMIM

A well-known acronym to help remember things that ought to be considered under resources is MEMMIM. It stands for:

Materials:	all types.
Environment:	including energy and waste, and services such as water, gas.
Manpower:	external and internal, including management.
Money:	budget allocation, contingency funds.
Information:	from people, books, databases, research.
Machinery:	including tools, computers, and vehicles.

The person

Who will you choose? Should it be the person best qualified for the task or someone who needs to learn new skills? The answer to that will depend on how much time is available, how urgent the task is, how important it is, how important you believe people development is, etc. Things you might consider include:

- ❑ Is your priority to develop staff or to clear an urgent job?
- ❑ Qualifications and experience, is the person capable of doing this job with or without training or coaching?
- ❑ Has he or she got the time, or can the time needed be freed up?
- ❑ Motivation level, will he or she apply themselves to the task?
- ❑ Is he or she being considered for promotion?
- ❑ Is this task already within the job description?
- ❑ Will the opportunity be welcomed?
- ❑ Will the training or coaching needed be welcomed and beneficial?
- ❑ How will the other team members react?
- ❑ How will the customer react if directly affected?

Plan your briefing meeting with the person. Where can you go that is quiet and you can talk easily? How will you introduce the topic?

Training

If the person is already capable of doing the task then obviously no training or coaching will be needed and you may expect the task to be completed reasonably quickly with little help from yourself. If the task will stretch the individual then some coaching may be needed, even if you send him or her on a training course first.

If this is a new area of expertise for the individual then you must be prepared to help considerably as an investment in his or her future and the future of your team. This may mean booking a formal training course or arranging for time to be spent with an acknowledged expert, or it may mean that all the learning will be prompted by coaching, ie helping the person to learn everything 'on the job'. Or it may be a mixture of these and other learning activities.

Whatever initial learning method you arrange, if any, you must also be ready to devote time to coaching, either yourself or through someone else. If the latter, it means someone else receiving a related delegated task: to coach the first person.

Responsibilities

People get confused over the meaning of jargon words like responsibility, accountability and authority, so think carefully about what you mean by these terms so that you do not baffle your staff with them. Responsibility and accountability mean much the same thing.

Your delegates are responsible to you for achieving the tasks, and for deciding how to do them. They are accountable to you for their actions. In other words, they answer or report or give account to you for their success in meeting the responsibilities they have accepted from you.

Meanwhile you are accountable to your manager for your own actions, including the fact that you have delegated tasks and some of your authority (see below) to members of your team. If it all goes wrong then your delegates answer to you and you answer to your boss. Ultimately you are in charge. Although they are doing the work you are accountable for the success because you delegated it.

A submarine returned to her home port after a voyage and the captain went on leave. The first lieutenant was left in charge with orders to clean the buoyancy tanks, a routine task that he had completed successfully many times before. This manoeuvre involves flooding and emptying the tanks, a process that tilts the submarine in the water first one way and then the other. The first lieutenant decided to leave hatch covers open to provide fresh air to the skeleton crew below deck. While not according to the rule book it was fairly common practice. A mistake was made and the bow was tilted down a little too far. The open hatch went under the water, the sea flooded in and the submarine sank. The captain was 100 miles away at the time but both the first lieutenant and the captain were court-martialled – the first for sinking the submarine and the second for leaving his ship in the charge of someone who sank it.

Learning point:
You are accountable to your manager for the success of everything you delegate to others.

Stop points

Build in stop points or safety nets at specific stages throughout the task before any major decision has to be made or any significant risk has to be taken, mainly so that you can check that everything is satisfactory before they proceed. The delegate is not authorized to proceed beyond a stop point until you say so. You might say, 'Consider the situation, come up with three possible courses of action and recommend one with your reasons why. Let me have that as a two-page report and then stop until we have discussed it.' Typically you would use stop points:

- ❑ Before committing significant expenditure.
- ❑ Before committing significant resources.
- ❑ Before involving other people, especially from outside your department.
- ❑ At regular stages so that if mistakes have been made they can be

corrected quickly before the effects become significant or difficult to correct.

- ❑ Before any major change or decision has to be made.

As you move higher up the scale of delegation levels, and delegate more authority for more important matters, you will need to choose your stop points or safety nets more and more carefully. The more experience delegates have, the fewer the number of stop points they are likely to want for a given task. Yet the more important the task is, the more stop points you will want to use.

The conundrum is that the more important tasks (where you want more stop points) are usually delegated to the more experienced delegates (who want fewer stop points). It is a fine balancing act. The skill lies in getting the number of stop points sufficient to give you the opportunity to prevent any serious problems building while leaving a good member of staff highly motivated by the challenging task in hand.

> During the American Apollo missions to the Moon in 1969–72 stop points were built into each mission at each major decision point. These included before committing to the launch, before leaving Earth's orbit, before entering lunar orbit, before detaching the lander from the command module, before descending towards the lunar surface, and before committing to the landing. Anyone who watched the missions live or has seen videos of them will remember the exciting phrase, 'You are go for…'
>
> **Learning point:**
> Build in stop points before every step that commits you to the next major stage of action or expenditure.

Authority

Authority is power. By giving authority to the delegates you empower them to do something such as take action, spend money, or commit resources on your behalf. The authority you give them will be limited (just as yours is) and it will be less than your own.

Normally you will authorize them to proceed up to the next stop point, spending no more than so much money or time, or using so much of a resource, etc.

The level of authority will reflect the three or six levels of delegation referred to in the last chapter (such as approval first, act and report, full authority) and may depend on the culture in your company. Your company may have rules that prohibit you from authorizing others to sign expenditure from your budget, for example.

In some companies acting without authority is a serious breach of discipline. In a few it is good use of initiative. Differences of approach can exist between different divisions within the same company or between different managers in the same division. It is wise to know where you stand and good practice to tell your delegates at the start how you see things. Often when someone acts without authority a manager will judge on a combination of outcome and intent, which can leave the judgement dependent on luck to a large degree. Staff then do not know where they stand and may see the manager as inconsistent. That is a dagger to the heart of good delegation.

In many companies a quick way to get into trouble is to talk to the press without authorization. A well-meaning engineer took a phone call and answered a few questions about a project he was working on. The next day a newspaper published a few things that the company would rather have kept quiet about and attributed them to a 'spokesperson'. The company now only allows named individuals to take press calls and has sent them on an external course called 'Handling the Press'.

Acting without authority is not new. King Henry II of England and Thomas à Becket, his Archbishop of Canterbury, had many strong disagreements. In December 1170, after Henry had again moaned about his 'turbulent priest' four of his knights took matters into their own hands and murdered Becket in his own cathedral.

Learning point:
Make certain your delegates understand the limits of their authority.

Reviews

Make it clear that these are not optional. You need reviews to keep you up to date because you are not abdicating your own responsibility. Whether you call them reviews, meetings or chats does not matter provided you build them in regularly. You will need them more frequently near the start of a project than later, and you will need them more often with someone who is new or who is being coached than with an experienced person. You will always need them at stop points. Use reviews to find out what has happened, which stage the project or task has reached, and (if satisfied) to authorize the individual to proceed to the next stop point.

Feelings

Listen to what your delegates tell you and probe to see how they feel about having tasks delegated to them. Not everyone will rush to thank you. You may have to give them time to think. Explain that you trust them to do this, promise them your support and be sure they believe you. Assure them that this includes backing them even if they make a mistake and taking responsibility for the mistake yourself – you will be supervising them after all. Give encouragement and explain why you have included stop points. They are there to prevent disasters. If they have not done this type of job before then you will devote time to coaching them. You are in it together. Get them to talk rather than just listen to you, they should do at least half the talking. Check that they understand what you are asking of them, including judging their own success. You will need to listen carefully and listening skills are discussed with other techniques in Chapter 9.

Refusal

If, in effect, they refuse your magnanimous offer of a delegated task then what do you do? Persuasion and negotiation techniques are discussed in Chapter 9 but before you try persuading or negotiating answer these questions, with them or on your own:

- ❑ Are they declining just this one delegated task, or all delegated tasks?
- ❑ If it is just this one, why precisely? What exactly are they afraid of? If you can alleviate that fear will they then accept the task? If not, there is some other fear, what is it? If you can answer that fear, will they then accept the task willingly?
- ❑ If you really cannot make progress what other task could you delegate to them instead? Who can you delegate this one to now?
- ❑ If they are refusing all new tasks, are they content to stay at their present level until they leave or retire? Can you accept that?
- ❑ If not, what is needed to help them to change their mind? Or to which department would they like a transfer?

Other people

Who else needs to be told? Possibly other members of your team will be wondering what is going on, especially if you have not been a delegator before. Tell them. You will be delegating things to them as well in due course. Also think about whether people outside your team need to know: your own boss, the internal or external customer, anyone whose co-operation is needed such as a storeperson or security guard. In some industries the trade union may need to be told.

Write it down

Once any reservations have been addressed and commitment is gained, agreement has been reached. Write it down so that there can be no future misunderstanding. Keep it as simple as you can but document the task with the outcomes or results required, the deadline, resources, training and coaching, stop points and so on. In effect this is the contract between you. To help you a sample planning sheet is provided at the end of this chapter. The more complex the task is, the more detail you will need to write down. With a simple task a verbal agreement may be acceptable but if in any doubt write it down so as to prevent any misunderstanding.

DURING

Once they have started work on the task, you stand back and let them get on with it while monitoring through regular reviews. Make sure they know that the standard must be achieved all the way through, no last-minute panic rushes. Encourage, watch and coach as necessary. Intervene as a last resort and then, if possible, intervene by questioning. If you are coaching as well as delegating you must make sure you have ample time for discussions and questions.

Stand back

It is now their task and their problem. Let them handle it. You have set the objectives to be achieved and the deadlines and the results needed, now give them the freedom to achieve them in their own way. Let them concentrate on the detail while you take in the wider scene. Poor delegators often start by telling their staff not just what the task is but how to do it as well, sometimes in great detail. That is a mistake. There is more about this in the chapter on coaching.

Avoid re-inventing the wheel

From time to time you will see that they are doing something that you know can be done better another way. While it is good to let them explore and find out things for themselves, and they may even come up with a better solution than you have, it is foolish to let them waste time up blind alleys that you definitely know go nowhere. Guide them and advise them. Lead them back out of the wilderness. Explain what is happening and suggest which way to go. Take a pragmatic approach but tread a careful path between telling them every step and leaving them completely in the dark.

Monitor and review

Avoid looking over their shoulder all the time. Instead make periodic checks on two types of information: the results and the methods. This enables you to look at both effectiveness (whether the right things are being done to the right standard) and efficiency (whether they are being done with least waste of time and effort). Do not confuse the two.

Always check interim results and time-scales as your main means of monitoring that satisfactory progress is being made, and make sample checks on the methods they are using so that you can satisfy yourself about the efficiency with which that progress is being achieved. Make these checks at every stop point and, at your discretion, between stop points. The skills of observing, listening, questioning and giving feedback are discussed in Chapter 9:

- *Effectiveness*: Results, interim results and time-scales tell you that progress is being made.
- *Efficiency*: Methods tell you about the efficient use of time and resources.

Authorize further progress

As stop points are reached, get direct feedback from the delegate by discussion and then decide whether to authorize progress to the next stop point. There may be other considerations as well, especially on a large project where this task is complete in itself but only one of many interacting tasks which involve other people. You, yourself, may require authorization to proceed further.

Question and coach

Always listen carefully to what your delegate has to tell you and probe carefully with questions (see Chapter 9). Always ask yourself if you can take things at face value. Things may not be as they seem. If this is also a learning exercise for this individual then coaching provides many opportunities to dig deeply into what is happening.

> A manager who had just joined a company asked a technician to investigate a technical problem and write a short report. When the manager checked for feedback he was told that all was going well and was given some technical details. Time went on but no report

> appeared. The deadline came and went. No written report ever appeared although a verbal one did. The new manager did not yet know his people. The technician could not bring himself to tell his new boss that he was quite incapable of writing a report.
>
> **Learning point:**
> You cannot always take things at face value. Probe deeper if unsure.

Intervene by questions

The less experience the individual has, the closer you will need to monitor his or her methods and interim results. This makes it more likely that you will spot a problem in the making.

If you do spot a problem brewing allow a little time to see if the individual will spot it and take corrective action. If time moves on and he or she is still oblivious to the situation then it is time to act, but how? Again there is not one answer but a scale of options open to you. These range from one extreme of stopping the action, to the other of casually asking how things are going. Use the least disruptive intervention possible and intervene by question if you can. In rising order of urgency:

- ❑ 'Can we talk about the situation in. . ?'
- ❑ 'What is happening in. . ? What will happen if this continues?'
- ❑ 'Do you think we might have a problem developing in. . ?'
- ❑ 'I think we have a problem developing in. . .'
- ❑ 'We definitely have a problem in. . .'
- ❑ 'Stop!'

Always move quickly if:

- ❑ Health and safety issues are involved.
- ❑ There are significant financial risks.
- ❑ There are sensitive aspects.
- ❑ A major customer is involved.

Difficult customers

If you know your delegates will have to deal with some difficult people then warn them. Tell them who is likely to be a problem to deal with, why, and what you know about them. What irritates them? What do they like? It is unfair and does nothing for your reputation if you send your delegate into the lion's den without preparation.

Taking over

Ideally you should never take over. Instead coach, guide, warn or tell. However, the pragmatist knows that in rare circumstances you may have to take over yourself, such as if very urgent action is needed or if there is a crisis and serious damage could result if the right action is not taken quickly. Such situations can be difficult to handle.

Your first action should be, with your delegate, to stop and think. If possible leave your delegate in charge but direct his or her actions. Only in rare circumstances should you take over publicly. Your first priority will be to mount the rescue but your second priority has to be to make sure your delegate is neither affronted nor demotivated. In many circumstances he or she may simply be grateful. Your third priority will be to hand back control to the delegate as soon as possible. The danger is that you start to enjoy the fun and hang on to the control and that is a mistake.

Be informal

Retain an informal but professional air in your relationship with your delegate. Let there be no shadow of doubt that you want the results delivered on time and to the standard agreed. Informality does not mean acting unprofessionally or lowering standards.

Keep records

Keep accurate records of the facts as you go along so that you can discuss progress in terms of facts rather than opinions. It is much easier to disagree about opinions than it is to disagree about facts. Depending on the company you may also need the facts for your end-of-year appraisal of performance.

AFTER

Assessment

When the task is completed then comes the time to assess and evaluate the performance properly, a stage that is often missed or done inadequately. This formal assessment is your opportunity to finalize your judgement about the success throughout the task, what went well and not so well, to discuss this with the delegate in a calm and unhurried manner, and to explore lessons learned and yet to be learned. It is a final grand review and follows the same principles as reviews.

Assessment need not be very formal and long-winded:

- ❑ First look at effectiveness. Allowing for any changes agreed along the way, were the actual results, both throughout and at the end, achieved to the standards and time-scales agreed?
- ❑ Then look at efficiency. Were the methods used the best available and was wastage kept to a minimum?
- ❑ The answers can only be largely yes or no although there are bound to be grey areas.

If yes:

- ❑ Thank and congratulate the people concerned.
- ❑ Praise them, in front of colleagues if appropriate.
- ❑ Reward them if appropriate.

Learning points you might discuss could include the following:

- ❑ Compare the original objectives and any agreed changes with the actual results. Were the original ones realistic? If not, could that have been foreseen? Who by?
- ❑ Discuss the methods used. Would you have used different methods? Discuss what and why.

- ❑ Explore the problems encountered and how they were solved.
- ❑ Would you have done anything else differently? What and why?

If no:

Thank them for what they have achieved and the efforts they made. Then discuss the following:

- ❑ What was and was not achieved? Treat the parts that were achieved as suggested above.
- ❑ Were things not achieved because they were impractical? When could this have been foreseen?
- ❑ Was there a misunderstanding or poor communication between you? How can that be prevented in the future?
- ❑ Was the person incapable of achieving the task? (This should never be discovered at the end. It should be discovered quite early on and action taken.)
- ❑ Was the training or coaching inadequate?
- ❑ Did circumstances change during the project and render it no longer required or feasible?
- ❑ Were the methods used inappropriate?
- ❑ Was your monitoring inadequate?
- ❑ What can be learned to prevent similar mistakes occurring in similar future projects or tasks?

Above all remember that the only people who never make mistakes are those who never do anything. Give praise for what went right and, together, learn from what went wrong. It is unlikely that a conscientious or professional person will deliberately fail.

Evaluation

Many people regard assessment and evaluation as the same thing, but evaluation adds one critical element. You have assessed what was achieved and how well it was achieved, now ask what difference has it made? What difference has it made to your team, department and to the organization? To what extent has it contributed to your department's or the organization's goals? It is a critical question and one that is often ignored.

Rewards

It is always possible for a manager to reward staff for a job well done because reward does not have to mean monetary reward. Most people welcome a genuine 'thank you' or a meaningful comment about a job well done. Normally these carry more weight if said in front of colleagues. However, some people would hate a public thank you although it may be acceptable at a local team meeting. Some managers are authorized to give small rewards such as gift tokens or a meal out. Rewards are discussed more fully in Chapter 9.

Rebuke in private

If a rebuke has to be delivered then do it as soon as possible after the event and do it in private. Be quite certain of your facts. Criticize the person's actions, not the person. Criticizing the person is totally unacceptable unless you are perfect yourself. Only use facts and do not get involved in an argument about opinions. You will never win an argument over opinions but the facts should be beyond dispute. If necessary set objectives for their behaviour and then put this incident behind you. Finish with positive comments about the things that went right.

> **Let your motto be, 'Catch them doing something right,' not, 'Catch them doing something wrong.'**

SWOT YOUR PERFORMANCE

Look back over the items listed for the Before, During and After phases of delegation. Do a SWOT analysis on how you actually perform when you delegate at the moment. Assess your own strengths and weaknesses as you currently see them. Try to assess the opportunities open to you to improve and the threats that may prevent you from improving.

Table 4.1 *SWOT analysis of your delegation skills*

	Strengths	Weaknesses	Opportunities	Threats
Before				
During				
After				

Then:

- ❑ Look at the weaknesses and decide which to improve and how.
- ❑ Look at the opportunities. When will be the next occasion you can try an improved method of delegation? What specific points will you improve? If you were delegating this improvement to someone else what would you set as the objective?
- ❑ Look at the threats. What problems might arise that could thwart your improvement plan? (For example, a personality clash with the person you are going to delegate to.) How can you lessen or eliminate the threat?

WHAT TO DELEGATE NEXT

Think about all the tasks that you perform. Use the list of what to delegate, given in the last chapter, and make out your own list of tasks that you could delegate to someone else. List everything that you find time-consuming, routine or repetitive.

Do not worry yet about who you will delegate to. Get the list of your possible tasks sorted first.

Then make a list of all your staff – everyone it is theoretically possible for you to delegate to. Ignore no one because of current conditions such as their workload or sickness. Write this list alongside the task list, as shown on p. 72.

Still ignoring current workload and such, draw lines to link tasks to people who could do them if the conditions were right. Pick your top three lines, the three most important to achieve. Perhaps these would bring the greatest saving of your own time, or the greatest benefit to the team as a whole, or the greatest benefit in developing a good member of staff.

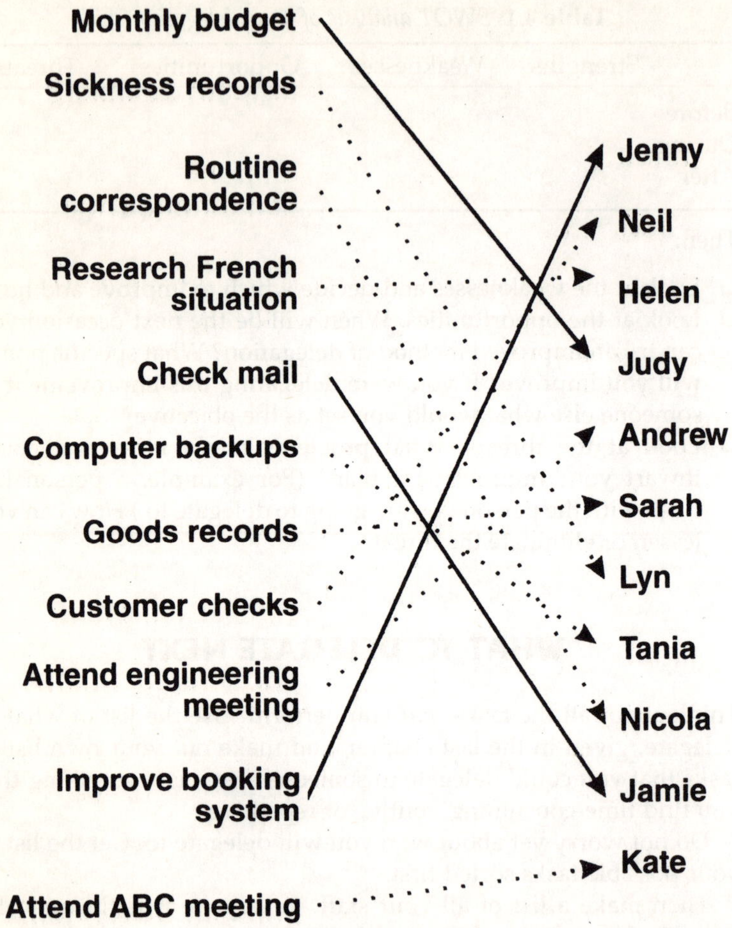

Figure 4.1 *Matching staff and tasks*

If any of these links are affected by conditions not being right, such as the person's workload, lack of knowledge and so on, decide now what you can do to correct this so as to make the delegation possible.

Finally, turn to the delegation planning sheet at the end of this chapter. Use it for ideas and adapt it to your own circumstances. Design your own planner and get to work.

CONCLUSION

Follow the steps in this chapter and your delegation skills will improve. There is a lot to be gained for you, for the delegate and for the department or company. Maximize those benefits by deliberately and methodically setting out to improve your delegation skills. Your greatest reward could be when your staff come to thank you for it.

In the next chapter we look at how to integrate the skill of coaching into your practice of delegation to form a seamless whole which, eventually, will become your normal way of working.

DELEGATION PLANNING SHEET

Define the task: *Outcomes/results required, standards to be achieved.*

Deadlines, time-scales:

The person:

Reason why: *Relation to departmental or company goals and business plan. How will you introduce the subject? What reaction might you expect?*

Resources needed: *Manpower, environment, material, money, information, machines.*

Training needed: *Formal courses, coaching, books, tapes, visit to expert, learning packages, etc.*

Level of authority delegated:

Level 1: Look into it.

Level 2: Suggest alternatives.

Level 3: Make recommendations.

Level 4: Start after I approve.	*Proceed to stop point.*	*Approval first.*
Level 5: Start before I approve.	*Proceed to stop point.*	*Act and report.*
Level 6: Do it all.	*Tell me later.*	*Full authority.*

Known stop points:

Monitoring: *Methods, frequency, meetings. Effectiveness and efficiency.*

Other people to tell:

5

PEOPLE AND LEARNING

When we defined coaching in Chapter 2 we noted that there can be problems in agreeing definitions. Different people produce different definitions but there are nearly always certain things they have in common. Things such as:

- ❑ Coaching is about developing staff.
- ❑ The person being coached is learning a new skill, usually in an effective and enjoyable way.
- ❑ It is not the same thing as training.
- ❑ It does not happen in a classroom or laboratory.
- ❑ The person being coached does the job while being coached.
- ❑ The coach is usually the manager or a colleague.
- ❑ The coach does not have to be the best there is at the subject.
- ❑ It is more than 'sitting with Nellie'.
- ❑ It works best when accompanied by delegation.
- ❑ It is a short-term investment for a long-term gain.
- ❑ It assumes that people have potential for far more than they currently achieve.
- ❑ Both the coach and the person being coached gain from the experience.
- ❑ It has side effects such as building rapport and encouraging teamwork.

Each of these statements has a ring of truth about it. Together they give an extensive, if unwieldy, picture of coaching that broadly agrees with the definition given in Chapter 2, which was: *Coaching is the provision of guidance and encouragement to help people to learn for themselves by doing the job.*

Let us look at some of these statements which were actually made by delegates on training courses. Is coaching really different from training? The answer to that can depend on your viewpoint because the two terms are often used loosely. For example, you hear of football coaches leading training sessions. A tennis coach is someone who charges you a hefty fee for tennis lessons, whereas tennis trainers are what you wear on your feet while having your expensive tennis lessons.

COACHING AND TRAINING

For the sake of distinguishing between them training and coaching can be differentiated as follows.

Training

- ❑ Takes place off-the-job.
- ❑ Is usually in a classroom, seminar room or training laboratory away from your normal place of work.
- ❑ Is conducted as a course, seminar or workshop.
- ❑ May be led by a professional trainer or someone who specializes in the subject.
- ❑ The trainer is not a member of your work group, except by chance.

Coaching

- ❑ Takes place on-the-job.
- ❑ Is usually at your normal place of work.
- ❑ Is integrated into the normal work and, when done best, is not distinguished as a separate special activity.
- ❑ Is led by your manager or a close colleague who will normally be a member of your work group.

So coaching is not training, but it can be used to support training or it can be used alone. Often a training course is the best answer to a learning need, but it should be followed routinely by delegation so that the individual can put what he or she has learned into practice.

The delegation should then be accompanied by coaching so that the individual can deepen still further his or her new knowledge and skill. In this way you can manage the process of converting the classroom learning into practical results. Training is not an end in itself and neither is coaching. Both contribute to the results.

This brings out another important difference between coaching and training. In coaching, because the learning is integrated into doing the work, what is learned is what is needed for the work you want them to do. Other scenarios, which may be discussed on a formal training course, are not necessarily brought into a coaching session. They can be but often they are not. Usually in coaching thoughts are focused on the job in hand rather than in providing an all round education on the subject. This can be a strength or a weakness depending on your viewpoint. Do you want your staff to consider things beyond the immediate or do you just want immediate effectiveness? When starting to coach someone be sure to consider whether you want to include any wider issues, even though they may not be needed at the moment.

Rapport

One further benefit of coaching over training is worth a mention before we leave the subject and that is the rapport and trust that it helps to build between the coach and the coached. Coaching a new member of staff is an excellent way of getting to know each other and learning to trust each other. Sending the person away on a training course will achieve things that coaching will not, but it will not achieve that personal rapport.

It is worth thinking about times when others have coached you and times when you have coached other people. You have probably received and given more coaching than you realize. Think back to when you learned to ride a bike. Which college did you attend?

It is a ridiculous question. You did not attend a course to be taught to ride a bike. You simply got onto the bike, tried to ride it and fell off. Then some kind person who had your interests at heart steadied the bike for you, even to the extent of running alongside with one hand holding the back of the saddle until finally having to let go because of no longer being able to keep up with you. He or she probably gave you advice and certainly gave you plenty of encouragement. When you finally rode off down the road, staying upright, that person took as much pleasure from your success as you did, even though you did not know it. If you look at our checklist above you will see that you were coached.

Later, as your confidence grew, you started to teach yourself to do things on that bicycle that your coach had never done, wheelies, bunny jumps and such things. Having been coached, you started to coach yourself – an under-valued benefit of coaching that companies largely ignore.

Have you ever watched a baby learn to walk? The new parents give enormous encouragement. They hold its hands as it struggles with its ill-developed sense of balance and movement. It watches other people walk and tries to imitate them. It learns on-the-job guided by its parents, in its normal living area and as part of the everyday process of growing. You were coached when you learned to walk.

You were coached when you learned to drive a car, one-to-one coaching while doing the actual job of real driving, except that this time you may have been coached by a professional driving instructor.

All of those were coaching experiences of one sort or another. But how would you learn to fly? In particular, how do people learn to fly jet aircraft? Before airline pilots are given jumbo jets to play with they learn the theory of flying the aircraft and they fly it in all kinds of situations on a simulator. In other words, they are trained, not coached.

BELIEF IN PEOPLE

Another delegate's remark recorded above was that coaching assumes that people have potential for more than they currently achieve. Coaches intrinsically take this view or they could not coach. One management guru once asked a question along the lines of: 'Why do some employers expect their workers to leave their brains in the locker room when they arrive for work and pick them up again on their way out?'

Thankfully, a coach does not. A coach expects the brains to be brought into work all polished up and ready for action and a coach is usually rewarded by the response. This stems from a situation of mutual trust and respect between a manager and his or her staff. If that situation is not already there then delegation and coaching with appropriate monitoring (especially the safety net of stop points) can start to build the trust and respect that is needed in modern management. Without it there is the rule by fear which is an indicator of what I call 'Jurassic Management'.

Signs of Jurassic Management:

- ❑ Staff have more fear of getting something wrong than eagerness to get it right.
- ❑ Managers like to 'catch them doing something wrong', rather than, 'catch them doing something right'.
- ❑ Managers use delegation as a trap.
- ❑ Managers throw people in at the deep end. 'If they drown, someone else will take their place.'
- ❑ Managers often criticize but rarely praise.
- ❑ Staff turnover is higher than the norm for that industry.
- ❑ Managers can chill a bottle of wine by entering the room.

Coaching, at its best, has gone beyond the stage where anyone thinks of it as coaching. It is just the natural way of working.

> **Think of examples, at work or elsewhere, when you have been coached well and examples of when you have been coached badly. What were the essential differences in what happened and how it happened? From these experiences, is there anything you would add to the bullet points above?**

HOW WE LEARN

Common sense tells us that a lot of what people learn about their job they learn while doing the job. It has been said that up to 90 per cent of an employee's development takes place on the job. No doubt the figure can be argued over but most people appear to accept that we learn most effectively by doing rather than being talked at, and that we learn a huge amount by doing our jobs.

As coaching is about directing thoughtful effort towards increasing learning while doing the job this suggests two things:

1. That managers play a crucial role in how much and how well their staff develop their knowledge, skills and attitudes.
2. That if managers understood how their staff learn then they would be better at coaching.

Without wishing to get lost in theory, it is therefore worth devoting some thought and effort to understanding what is known about how people learn. Many people have studied this and some of their practical conclusions are summarized below.

KOLB LEARNING CYCLE

Everyone learns from experience. Many only learn to cope and this may require little thought. They simply pick things up as they get on with life. Trial and error teaches you which drink you prefer from the coffee machine. That is learning to cope, but not learning so that you can improve things. Others, however, seem to think harder about situations and look for ways to change things, to improve them – they learn in order to improve.

So, there are two types of learning from experience:

1. Learning so as to cope.
2. Learning so as to improve.

It is learning so as to improve that we want to encourage by coaching.

David Kolb has described learning by experience, learning to improve things, as a cycle:

- ❑ You do or experience something.
- ❑ You think about or reflect on it, question it, review the experience.
- ❑ You draw some conclusions about it and generalize it.
- ❑ You decide what to do next time and experiment with the plan.

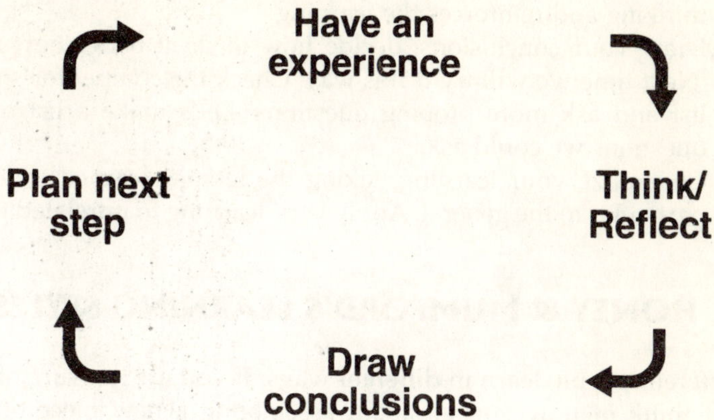

Figure 5.1 *Kolb Learning Cycle*

What use is this to you as a manager?

While this learning cycle may seem self-evident (usually after someone has pointed it out to you) several action points can be drawn from it once you start to think about it.

Action

- ❑ Tell your staff that you expect them to learn so as to improve, not so as to cope. You want continuous improvement.
- ❑ Delegate more. They cannot learn from experience if you will not let them have experiences to learn from.
- ❑ Look for learning opportunities for yourself and your staff. Coach them, 'You saw the visitor from Company X, did you explore outside their normal terms of business?'
- ❑ Ask more questions. Encourage everyone to review and question what they have done. With the pressures of work this can seem an impossible task – actually stopping the doing in order to think. Take just a few minutes and you will reap benefits. It will rarely need to be longer if it is done frequently. ('With that visitor, what other questions could you have asked? Did you check the price list from Company Y?')

- ❑ Write down what you have learned. Writing clarifies your thinking and reinforces the learning.
- ❑ Draw your conclusions; decide how to do it better next time. 'Next time we will try it this way: Check the competitor's price list and ask more probing questions. Let's make a list of the questions we could ask.'
- ❑ Generalize your learning, taking the lessons learned from the particular to the general. Apply your learning to unrelated tasks.

HONEY & MUMFORD'S LEARNING STYLES

Different people learn in different ways. If you are not sure of that just think of how you go about assembling a new piece of DIY furniture. Some people lay out every part on the carpet, arranged in sequence as shown in the instructions, and they read the instructions carefully from cover to cover. Others assemble it by trial and error, only using the instruction leaflet to protect the carpet from the glue.

Peter Honey and Alan Mumford suggested that there are four basic styles of learning. Each style has its advantages and disadvantages and we all use all four styles but not equally. We may have a strong preference for one or two particular styles or we may mix three or four fairly evenly. They devised a lengthy and now widely used questionnaire to identify preferences. Check if your organization uses it because you will find it helpful to determine your own preferred learning style and those of your staff.

How do you think you learn best? Arrange these four statements in descending order of your preference:

- ❑ I like to plunge straight in, get on with it and see what develops.
- ❑ I like to take my time, thinking things through carefully.
- ❑ I like to read about the matter and study and explore it before doing anything.
- ❑ I like to make it happen, learn from others and get the result.

What sequence do you think applies to you?

Honey and Mumford defined these styles as: Activist, Reflector, Theorist and Pragmatist.

The value of understanding the styles is that they can help you to improve your coaching by allowing you to match the methods you use to the preferred learning styles of your subordinates. You will make their learning more difficult if you use an approach that is strongly different from their natural style. For example, lending someone a book to read may be very helpful to a theorist but of little help to a strong activist. If you, yourself, are a strong theorist you may be puzzled as to why they ignore the book.

People's learning styles are reflected in their general behaviour, therefore observing their behaviour can give you an insight into their preferred learning styles. A brief summary of the behaviours associated with the four extremes is given here but full descriptions are provided with the questionnaire. Remember that different people embrace different amounts of each style.

Activists

Activists tend to be fully involved in the here and now, enjoying new experiences and the excitement and drama of crises. They dive in rather than stand back and would rather be players than observers. They may ignore rules and may not see things through to the final details. They do not relish lectures, reading, long explanations and precise instructions, preferring to be in the limelight by doing now and thinking later.

Reflectors

Reflectors prefer to stand back and think about things, collecting data and analysing it before taking action. They avoid the limelight and like things orderly with good instructions and no panics. They may be cautious, preferring to listen and learn before contributing. They give painstaking attention to detail, avoid taking the lead and rarely jump to conclusions.

Theorists

Theorists enjoy logical theories with things neat and complete. They will analyse and synthesize from complex data and produce elegant step-by-step models, testing assumptions and logic. They do not like subjectivity or lack of structure, preferring policies, procedures and intellectual rigour. They may not like working with many activists and may be perfectionists.

Pragmatists

Pragmatists want to know if it works in practice. They like to experiment and take on new challenges, preferring practical results to intellectual discussion. They will learn from the expert, try it out and prove it in practice; avoiding things with no immediate application or outcome worth pursuing. They are down to earth.

Now the activist in you will already have reached some conclusions about some of those you know: 'Charles is a theorist if ever I saw one, and Karen is a reflector.' The theorist will be saying, 'Fascinating. Where can I get the original?' The reflector will still be thinking about it while the pragmatist will already have asked, 'So what? What use is it?'

If you can recognize the combination of styles inherent in each of your staff and try to use a coaching method that will suit their combination then you will be a more successful coach. For example, if you ask someone how to do something in your word processor, such as set up tabs or tables, the person who leaps up and comes to your machine to show you is an activist. That person may well do it for you there and then, at a high speed, and leave you with it set up but little the wiser as to how it happened. The theorist will explain the structure of the software and pass you a book while the reflector may ask you what you have tried so far. The pragmatist will tell you about the short cut.

It is usually appropriate to involve several styles in your coaching because no one uses only one learning style. Suppose there is a new piece of machinery for people to operate. You could:

❑ Give them the manual	Theorists
❑ Discuss it with them carefully	Reflectors
❑ Demonstrate how to use its	Pragmatists
❑ Ask them questions about its	Theorists/Reflectors
❑ Let them 'play' with it	Activists/Pragmatists

Even better you could use all of these methods, starting with an explanation and demonstration and then leaving them with the manual and the machine so that they can read and experiment. Finally, you could return to see how they were doing and ask them questions. (Note: depending on what the machine is, safety issues may dictate a different course of action.)

A branch of the Civil Service was privatized and sold to a private sector company. Many of its managers had been civil servants for 20 years or more and had no direct experience of working in the private sector. The new owner saw an urgent need to transform a loss-making unit into a profitable one and set a three-year target. Many of the ex-civil servants believed sincerely that it was not possible to make a profit from their business and felt that the new management would eventually come to understand this. Needless to say, the new management did not agree. Everyone was clear as to what had to happen and by when, the real question was: how?

The divisional manager called a planning meeting of his senior team, a mix of ex-civil servants and others. The ex-civil servants came expecting to be told 'The Grand Plan', how they were to work this miracle. They were theorists: tell us how to do it, show us the rules and we will try. The divisional manager had different expectations. He came looking for mutual problem-solving, new ideas and action. He was a pragmatist and an activist.

Three years later the unit met its target but most of the senior ex-civil servants had left through redundancy or early retirement and had been replaced by others.

Learning point:
Use your delegates' strengths but develop their weaker styles to suit circumstances.

Here are some ideas to help you to develop weak styles of learning:

To strengthen the activist style of learning:

- ❑ Delegate tasks that need quick action and lots of enthusiasm.
- ❑ Put them in charge of something, such as chairing a meeting or leading a group.

To strengthen the reflector style of learning:

- ❑ Get them to explain their thinking to you before they act.
- ❑ Give them a problem and ask for a short thoughtful report with pros and cons for three courses of action.

To strengthen the theorist style of learning:

- ❑ Ask them to reduce a complex process to a flow diagram so that others can learn from it.
- ❑ Get them to analyse something that went wrong and identify when and why it started to go wrong, and how that can be prevented in the future.

To strengthen the pragmatist style of learning:

- ❑ Give them a task that must work.
- ❑ Ask them to coach someone at something they do well or write a short 'How to' instruction for some new machinery.

Action:

- ❑ Identify your preferred learning style(s) and those of your staff.
- ❑ Play to their preferred styles when coaching.
- ❑ Look for ways to strengthen their, and your, weaker styles in the long term.

HIERARCHY OF LEARNING

The final item of learning theory helps you to picture where your team members are in terms of both their competence at a skill and their awareness of their competence at that skill. Again, it is widely used and, while using tongue-twisting expressions, it is quite simple.

At the lowest level we do not possess the skill (we are incompetent but not in a derogatory sense) and are not even aware that a skill is needed. A young child gives no thought to what is involved in driving a car and may think it can do it. This is called unconscious incompetence.

At the next stage we know more about what is involved and the problems posed but we also know that we are not skilled in the area. People about to learn to drive or struggling to learn a new language fit into this category. They know they cannot do it yet. This is called conscious incompetence. Adults have many issues in this category, maybe things that you have tried, say skiing, but at which you are not skilled.

The next stage is when we are getting skilled at the task but have to give it our full concentration if we are to succeed. Someone approaching their driving test, a skier who falls if he or she looks at the scenery. This is conscious competence. We are competent provided we give it our full concentration.

Finally we are an expert, or at least very competent at the skill. We can drive and hold a conversation at the same time. We travel 50 miles along a motorway without thinking about it. We think in the foreign language as well as speak it. We have achieved unconscious competence. The skier is highly skilled and enjoys the views, the sun and the presence of other skiers as well as the run.

What use is this model to you? It provides you with a simple model (despite the language) to help you to judge where people are in terms of their levels of awareness and skill, and it gives you an indication of what to improve and how.

For example, in Figure 5.2:

- ❑ Box 1: They do not recognize that they cannot do the job properly. Explain the facts of life. Bring about the dawn of realization by comparing their achievements with those of others. Gain their willingness to improve or divert them to other work.
- ❑ Box 2: They know they are not skilled but are willing to learn. Coach and delegate if increasing their skill will be useful.
- ❑ Box 3: They can do it if they concentrate. Delegate and monitor. Give them opportunities to practice. If they only need to do this task occasionally (such as for sick cover) do they really need to get any better?

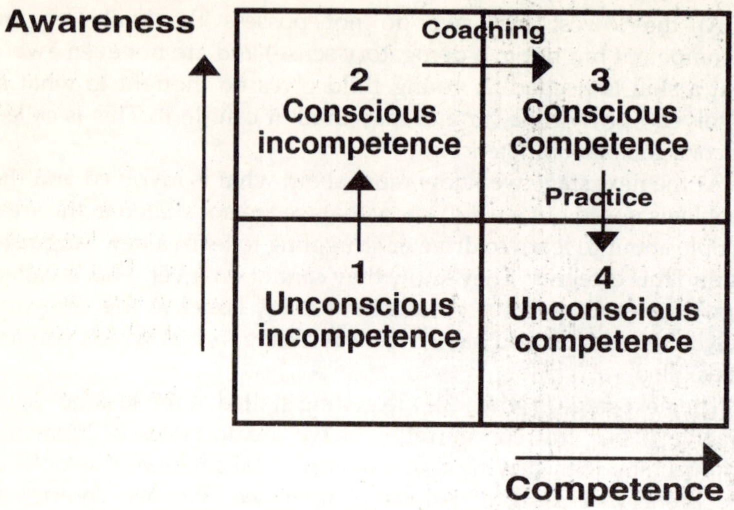

Figure 5.2 *The hierarchy of learning*

- ❑ Box 4: They can do it without thinking. Delegate. Get them to coach others.

CONCLUSION

The Kolb Learning Cycle may seem self-evident but if it is a simple concept let us use it. Things do not have to be complicated to be useful. Help your staff and yourself to question actions for a few minutes every day. Reflect so that you think, learn and plan. Encourage everyone to learn so as to improve rather than just to cope. Learn more about the learning styles and make use of preferred styles when you coach. Delegate small tasks to develop neglected styles. Finally, use the hierarchy of learning to spot opportunities for both coaching and delegating. Be careful with that word incompetent though, in common usage it has a strong derogatory tone that you must avoid. If in doubt call it lack of skill.

6

MOTIVATION

To state the obvious, if you are going to coach someone successfully it helps enormously if that person wants to learn. So what motivates someone to want to learn and what can you do to increase that motivation?

If you are a theorist you could spend weeks studying motivation theories. There are many theories which expound many views and which have built on previous theories. It is a very complex subject but some understanding of the basics can be useful to a manager. We will very briefly review four of the most popular theories, which collectively will help you to understand motivation a little better, and we will use examples in this and later chapters to illustrate the theories in action at work. In all of this however, remember that:

- Everyone is unique.
- People come from different social settings and therefore have different expectations which influence how they react.
- Society changes over time and what may have been a strong motivator for many people 20 years ago may be a lot weaker now.
- People change as they get older. What motivates people in their twenties may not do so when they are in their fifties.

THEORIES X AND Y

Douglas McGregor's Theories X and Y were mentioned briefly in Chapter 1. He suggested that there are two extremes in the way managers treat people, X and Y.

Theory X managers act as if people:

- ❑ Are lazy, dislike work and will avoid it if they can.
- ❑ Have to be coerced, directed, threatened and given incentives.
- ❑ Avoid responsibility, have little ambition and desire stability.
- ❑ Are indifferent to the needs of the company.

Theory Y managers act as if people:

- ❑ Find work natural, are self-motivated and self-controlled.
- ❑ Given satisfactory conditions, find work a source of satisfaction and enjoy achieving results.
- ❑ Learn to accept responsibility, even to seek it, and work best when given it and the freedom to achieve.
- ❑ Can contribute more than is usually recognized and have talents that are under-utilized.

The conclusions you can draw from McGregor and subsequent work is that your staff will reflect the way you treat them. If you treat them as work-shy, or if you withhold interesting work from them, you are hardly likely to motivate anyone and so you will 'prove' you are right. If you treat them as responsible adults and give them responsibility, most will respond positively. As someone put it, 'If you want people to do a good job, give them a good job to do.' The action for you is to delegate more, share your responsibilities. Let decisions be taken at the lowest level.

A senior engineer was passed over for promotion and subsequently started to receive criticism from his senior manager. He was told that he was not a team player, that he was too much of an individual and that he had made too many mistakes. His professional competence was criticized. It was the first time in ten years that he had received anything but praise. Suddenly he was given written targets to meet instead of setting his own, and had to answer to the man who had just been promoted who until very recently had been his peer. Before long he was reduced to abdicating total responsibility for his own decisions. 'Just tell me what you want me to do and I'll do it.'

Learning point:
Switching management style from Y to X demotivates people.

MASLOW'S HIERARCHY OF NEEDS

Abraham Maslow proposed a model of people's needs and arranged them in a hierarchy of ascending order. The basic idea was that people are motivated according to the level of needs at which they are operating. When one set of needs is satisfied it ceases to be a motivator and the manager should address the next higher set.

In ascending order these needs are:

- *Physiological*: the requirements for life – food, shelter, warmth, clothing, sexual satisfaction, sleep.
- *Safety and security*: freedom from physical threat and other physical, mental and emotional threats.
- *Social*: feelings of belonging, loving and being loved, being part of a group, family life.
- *Esteem*: esteem and respect from oneself and from others.
- *Self-actualization*: develop own gifts and talents to their full potential, accomplish something of importance.

While some argue with Maslow's model it has proved itself easy and useful in practice, even though life is far more complex than a simple understanding of the model might appear to proclaim. People do not simply work their way from satisfying physiological needs up to self-actualization, calling in at three stations on the way. Nevertheless it does help managers to grasp some understanding of what is happening in their team.

Delegating work to people is a strong motivator. At a minimal level it confirms their safety and social needs (they are obviously still wanted and part of things) and moves them up into esteem and self-actualization (they are recognized as valued employees and are being asked to accomplish something of importance).

Coaching is also a motivator, confirming the social needs of relationships and building the esteem needs of self-respect (I am learning something new and useful).

Maslow's model can sometimes help us to recognize why things are going wrong. In the case study recounted above the senior engineer had, at least in his own eyes, been operating at or near the top of Maslow's hierarchy. His esteem had been high and he had been accomplishing worthwhile things. Being passed over for

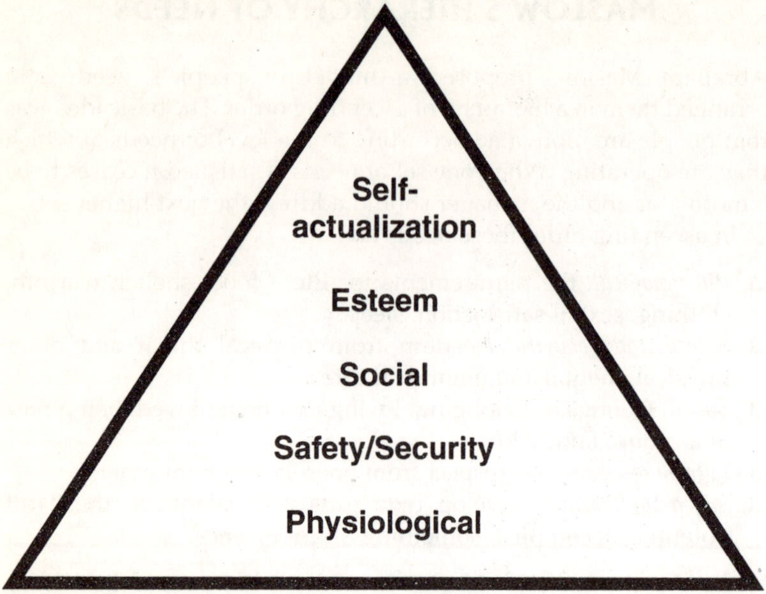

Figure 6.1 *Maslow's Hierarchy of Needs*

promotion attacked him at the esteem level and the subsequent criticism of his work and the loss of the privilege of setting his own targets compounded this. These attacked him at the esteem and social levels – he had lost his sense of belonging and his place in the group. His safety and security were also under threat. In a matter of weeks he had tumbled down the pyramid from level five to level two and switched into a totally defensive mode of working.

In western society most people's basic physiological needs are met either through their salary or wages or through forms of social security. It was not true a century ago and is not true today in many developing countries. Most managers have little influence over the base level, but the other four levels can be greatly affected by management style.

Many companies today demand increased loyalty, commitment, initiative and empowerment from their staff while at the same time getting 'leaner and fitter' by stripping out layers of management and making long-serving people redundant at all levels of the workforce. Meanwhile they announce business success after business success. This sends very confusing messages to their people – in Maslow's model at least.

Such policies, which are and have been very common in business life, demand self-actualization while breaking up teams (social needs) and threatening safety needs (the mental and emotional strain of seeing colleagues made redundant and wondering if you will be the next). They want their workers to sit on the roof of Maslow's hierarchy while they busily demolish the floors below.

So what can you as a manager do about this?

Maslow's model presents people's the needs as a simple hierarchy, each built on top of the last. If you damage the base then you damage them all and there is much truth in that, as many employees will testify. However, if instead we picture the needs as being mutually supportive, more like a set of pillars which collectively support us, then we can start to see a way forward in this modern dilemma. As one pillar is damaged, the others bear the load and can be strengthened until the first is repaired. It may be that the basic need (physiological) is not a pillar, but the plinth on which the other four pillars stand.

As an example that life is not as simple as Maslow's model might suggest, consider that for some people the social need to belong to a group, to love and to be loved, is as fundamental as the need for safety and security. For many refugees, their safety and security needs are threatened but love and social bonding is strong.

Picturing Maslow as a set of pillars instead of a pyramidal hierarchy suggests that, as a manager, you need to support all five levels to a greater or lesser degree *all the time* if your staff are to perform at their best. It is not simply a case of building up the levels one by one.

You are not going to change company policies in terms of what is required from staff in the new order of things. What you can do, however, is to recognize that when some basic needs are threatened you can use the demands placed upon you to achieve more with less as a route to compensating for some, but not all, of this threat.

If your staff feel their job security is threatened (safety and security) then try to compensate by increasing their esteem and self-actualization. Probably the best way to achieve this is to help them to increase their employability within your organization, and outside it if need be, by building their knowledge and skills and behaviours. Increased delegation and the coaching that goes with it are very effective ways of doing this. Nothing totally compensates for the threat of redundancy but the knowledge that your skills are fully up to date helps you to face an uncertain future with more confidence. When one set of Maslow's needs are threatened, strengthen the others.

HERZBERG'S TWO FACTOR THEORY

Another very helpful theory was suggested by Frederick Herzberg. Again, like Maslow, it has both an immediate ring of truth about it and is genuinely useful to a working manager.

Herzberg based his conclusions on the answers to questions put to thousands of employees and concluded that there are two sets of factors at play: those which demotivate if they are missing and those which motivate if they are present. You will see both in action around you. He called these the *hygiene* or *maintenance factors* and the *motivating factors*.

Hygiene factors

Provided these are in place and satisfactory then their effect on employees is neutral. But if they are unsatisfactory they cause dissatisfaction and problems. Like medical hygiene they prevent a deterioration rather than provide a cure. This can be irritating to senior managers, and to you as a manager, if they or you have struggled hard to get these things right only to see no appreciation of that fact, but that is life. Hygiene factors include:

- ❑ *Company policies and administration*: how well the business is managed.
- ❑ *Supervision*: the quality of the immediate management, fairness.
- ❑ *Interpersonal relationships*: especially in the team itself.

- ❑ *Working conditions*: the physical environment, appearance, tools available.
- ❑ *Salary*: including bonuses, perks, etc. Not seen as a motivator but as a demotivator if unsatisfactory.
- ❑ *Status*: the regard shown to the individual.
- ❑ *Job security*: including contractual agreements, fairness of redundancy package.

Motivating factors

These items give satisfaction and arise out of the job. They increase motivation and output.

- ❑ *Achievement*: the personal satisfaction associated with the job, success directly attributable to you.
- ❑ *Recognition*: including praise from manager and colleagues.
- ❑ *The work itself*: the challenge and interest it generates.
- ❑ *Responsibility*: the amount of control you have over what you do and how you do it.
- ❑ *Development/Advancement*: opportunities to gain new knowledge and skills, develop potential and advance your career.

You will see that Herzberg's motivating factors are strongly influenced by the local manager. A manager who is good at delegating, coaching and praising staff is giving strong support to all the motivational factors. Such managers make jobs more interesting, praise their staff when they do things well and give them more responsibility, all of which build personal satisfaction. People develop through coaching and doing new things, expand their experience and eventually open up prospects for their advancement.

Think back to the case study of the senior engineer. When his manager detected problems and wanted to correct these and motivate a previously valued member of staff the manager's actions had the opposite effect. Why? Because every one of Herzberg's motivational factors were removed (achievement, recognition, some of the work, responsibility and advancement) and four of the hygiene factors were damaged (supervision, interpersonal relationships, status and job security). Was it any wonder that the senior engineer became demotivated?

ARGYRIS'S MATURITY THEORY

Clive Argyris suggested that apathy and lack of effort might be normal healthy reactions from mature and psychologically healthy people to an unhealthy industrial situation of bureaucracy and formality. In these terms the biggest enemy to motivation is how companies organize themselves.

Argyris argued that people can develop to achieve their highest potential, to be fully responsible, acting with self-reliance and independence, and that the organization then benefits just as much as the individual. However, many organizations are structured to prevent this from happening. They actually require immature behaviour from employees and make them dependent on authority. Examples include excessive checking before action can be confirmed, and multiple signatures to authorize the purchase of inexpensive items. Argyris's message at its simplest is: treat your staff as mature and responsible adults instead of immature and irresponsible children.

In one organization all staffing questions were referred to the divisional manager for a decision. In a division employing many hundreds of people the divisional manager chaired every selection interview panel, even for temporary typists. In this instance managers were treated like immature and irresponsible children.

A company with about 50 branches was taken over by a rival. Among other things branch managers were responsible for the maintenance and repair of complex equipment. They had no budget responsibility and only had authority to spend £25 without higher approval. One of the first actions by the new owners was to increase this to £500 and make the branch managers responsible for their own budgets. The branch managers welcomed this. It increased their motivation as well as their authority because the new owner treated them as mature and responsible adults.

ACTION

Think about both the way you are managed and the way you manage your staff. What motivates or demotivates you and your staff?

A company decided to reorganize and appointed a project team to look at the current situation and make proposals. They were authorized to question anyone in the company but told not to discuss their findings. After many months the project team thought they were doing a great job but the previously happy workforce were moaning and fearful. The project team were treated according to Theory Y, the workforce according to Theory X. For the project team Herzberg's motivating factors were increased while the workforce perceived their hygiene factors to be threatened. Maslow's social and self-esteem needs were enhanced for the project team, while the workforce began to feel that their safety and security level was under threat. Open communication and more staff involvement could have prevented a breakdown of trust.

7

COACHING STYLES

Coaching is not an event, and most emphatically it is not a single event. It is an attitude of mind, a style of managing. It is not something to be switched on and off. You are not a coach if one day you decide to 'do a bit of coaching today'. As a management style it is like breathing. Would you one day decide to 'do a bit of breathing today'?

Coaching is part of a manager's job and an increasingly important part of it. It is so much a part of management style that some people say you do not have to be an expert at a subject to be able to coach it well. It is certainly true that a coach does not have to be the best at a subject in order to coach someone else. Think of top golfers who rely heavily on their coaches. If the coach was actually better at the game than the player would it not be the coach who was winning the millions of dollars prize money?

So coaching is a style of management. At its best it is automatic, with the coach acting in unconscious competence mode. It takes place without a special decision by the manager to 'start coaching' although, as you will see, there is conscious effort to enact the phases of coaching.

It requires a one-to-one relationship between the coach and the person being coached, a level of mutual trust and respect, a commitment to spend time on the process and an expectation that everyone will want to perform to the best of their ability for the common good. That brings us back to the more positive aspects of the theories of motivation: McGregor's Theory Y, Maslow's levels of esteem and self-actualization, Herzberg's motivating factors and Argyris's removal of barriers to allow employees to perform at their best.

STYLES

There are many styles of coaching. In fact there is a continuum which stretches from one extreme of on-the-job training, tell-show-do, to the other extreme of coaching by questions where individuals learn for themselves although guided by the coach. Many people regard the latter as true coaching.

Coaching is a mass of variables and to be pedantic about how a certain person should be coached and by what method is to invite problems. The best coaching method to use depends on many variables, including:

- ❑ The ability and experience of the individual.
- ❑ The attitude of the individual, to being coached and to learning itself.
- ❑ Previous experiences of being coached, positive or negative.
- ❑ His or her expectations.
- ❑ Preferred learning styles.
- ❑ The complexity of the task.
- ❑ The urgency.

The variation in coaching styles can be illustrated by describing the two extremes. Both are excellent at facilitating learning and are very successful in the right circumstances but neither is applicable to all situations. Between these two extremes lies a continuum that you can explore by mixing the two to various degrees.

For both styles a variety of skills are needed similar to those needed for delegation, such as listening, observing and asking questions, and these are explored in Chapter 9.

TELL-SHOW-DO

The tell-show-do method is a traditional method that assumes the coach is an expert and that there is a standard best method of doing the task. It is really training, although managers often use it on-the-job as coaching. If you have ever served in the armed forces you will have been coached this way when you learned to march or learned to shoot. It is used to train apprentices on the job and a lot of

Table 7.1 *Extremes of coaching styles*

TELL-SHOW-DO	COACHING BY QUESTIONS (OR BY EXPLORATION)
Leans towards training	*Definitely coaching*
Junior, less experienced staff	Senior, more experienced staff
Simpler tasks	Complex tasks
Standard method available	No standard method available
Lots of practice possible	Little practice possible
Little time available	More time available
Slower learners	Faster learners
Less retained	More retained

children learn domestic skills, such as how to make a pot of tea, this way. It is a case of, 'This is how you do it. Watch me. Now you do it.' It is very effective given the right circumstances.

The technique is straightforward.

Tell

Describe and explain the process of how to do the task and any supporting information that is needed, including health and safety issues. Question the individual to test understanding and ask for the process to be explained in his or her own words. Observe behaviour and body language for signs of interest, unease or boredom.

Show

Demonstrate the process by doing it yourself, probably with a running commentary as you progress so as to add depth and detail to the earlier description and explanation. Make it as clear and easy to follow as you can. Ask questions and observe the individual's reaction. Frowns and puzzled looks probably indicate loss of understanding. Moving to get a better view indicates both concentration and a need for you to make things more visible. In many situations the demonstration will have to be repeated, perhaps with variations.

Do

Get the individual to do the task, the first time with no pressures of time or accuracy. Allow mistakes to be made without criticizing and let the person talk you through them. Ask 'Is that right?' rather than saying 'You've got that wrong.' Focus on the process rather than on the person. At this stage ask questions rather than give the answers. Give plenty of encouragement and praise. If appropriate, such as if there are no safety hazards, let the individual practice alone and experiment with variations especially if he or she is an activist or pragmatist. At the end make sure the task can be performed competently and that he or she can talk you through it with confidence.

Two advantages of this method, essentially a teaching method, are that it usually achieves the objective of helping the individual to learn relatively quickly and it reinforces the learning by repeatedly doing the task. The degree to which the learning 'sticks' depends on how much the individual actually does and it will, generally, not be as high as is achieved by the questioning or exploration method, hence the need to keep practising. It is particularly useful with more junior staff, or those with little experience, and it is applicable to tasks that are not very complex and can be reduced to a flow of steps. It uses all four learning styles although reflection needs to be encouraged through good questions. Strong activists may have to be encouraged to listen and observe before being allowed to leap into the doing.

The tell-show-do approach has some variations:

Learning by drill

This is based on the tell-show-do method except that the 'do' element is repeated *ad nauseam* so as to 'drill' in the learning and improve the skill. We have all learned many things this way, from multiplication tables to some sports movements. In its higher form it is simply called practice.

Buddy system

The buddy system is a process where the learner is attached to an experienced member of staff and accompanies that person for a time. It is often used in small companies and is a useful method of 'inducting' a new recruit into the company, a time when there are a lot of new things to learn. For its success it depends entirely on the willingness, knowledge and skill of the buddy. The new person will learn from the buddy, warts and all. It can be very successful if used in a structured way with a planned sequence of activities that covers all agreed situations. Without a structured approach the chances of success are much diminished.

Sitting with Nellie

Very similar to the buddy system but more often used to learn a specific skill or set of skills. The learner is again attached to a buddy (Nellie) who is an acknowledged expert. The learner follows, observes and copies the way Nellie operates. Tell-show-do is used with lots of questions. Again it is effective if the tasks are relatively straightforward and Nellie is competent and uses the correct methods. As with the buddy system, from which at times it is indistinguishable, bad habits can be learned just as effectively as good ones. It works best if:

- ❑ Nellie builds a good rapport with the learners and has sympathy for them.
- ❑ Nellie can see the problems from the learner's view and has not forgotten what it is like to be a learner.
- ❑ Nellie has learned how to train and has some patience.
- ❑ Nellie is good at asking questions, listening to the answers and probing them.
- ❑ Nellie is given the time, the resources and the support to do the coaching properly.
- ❑ The learner has the opportunity to do the job or task.
- ❑ There are clear objectives to be met.

> Teaching a family member to drive is a common sitting-with-Nellie way of learning. As driving, driving conditions and the driving test have grown more complex there has been a shift towards more people being taught by professional driving instructors. This has been encouraged in part by the number of people who learned bad habits from experienced drivers that subsequently caused them to fail the tougher driving test. It is still mainly sitting with Nellie, but Nellie is now a professional coach.

COACHING BY QUESTIONS

This is sometimes called coaching by discovery or coaching by exploration and many people regard this as true coaching, seeing tell-show-do and its variations as training. The individuals learn by being given opportunities to explore issues and situations for themselves while doing the job and having clear goals to achieve, so that they discover the routes to success for themselves. The coach avoids telling and showing in favour of observation and feedback and above all, skilful questioning. The coach provides encouragement and guidance but the guidance is provided through the art of asking questions and giving feedback.

Doing is now central to the process instead of being the third of three stages as in tell-show-do. In fact the doing and questioning and feedback interact as much as possible so that, diagrammatically, the process has the questioning and feedback running alongside the doing and nudging its direction. Pictorially, it is reminiscent of a small tugboat nudging a large ship into dock, each nudge being a question or comment.

The art of questioning is a skill that needs considerable practice to develop. The general idea of the questions is to prompt the learners into exploring issues in depth either by direct questions or by implied questions – even a raised eyebrow – so that they become more aware of what is going on and can eventually coach themselves and others. Feedback can then be used to discuss

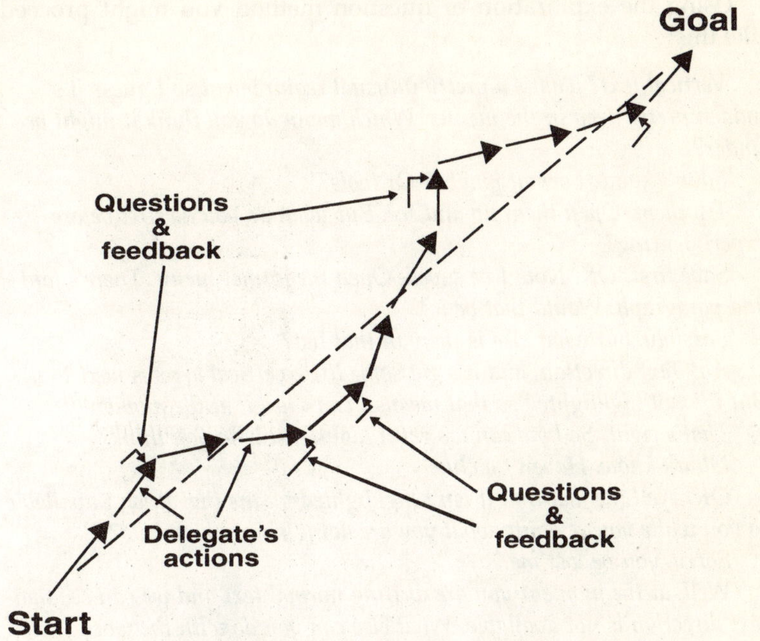

Figure 7.1 *Coaching by questions*

progress and provide guidance, but still by using questions as the main vehicle for progress whenever possible.

With a delegated task the safety nets of regular monitoring, feedback and stop points would be built in as discussed earlier.

Suppose someone wanted help with word processing, for example. Let's say he or she wanted to put some vertical text into the script instead of all horizontal text. How would you react?

One way would be to simply do it for that person – no coaching taking place there. Another way would be to use the tell-show-do approach. Learning will take place but, because vertical text is used so rarely, there is unlikely to be much reinforcement of this learning. The individual will do it this once and probably forget how it was done. Next time he or she will remember that it can be done but is likely to be frustrated by not remembering how to do it.

Using the exploration or question method you might proceed like this:

'Vertical text? That's a pretty unusual requirement so I guess it's hidden pretty deep in the menus. Which menu do you think it might be under?'

'I don't know. Format maybe? Or tools?'

'Try them. Open them up and see. But what do you do first before experimenting?'

'Save first. OK. Now I've saved. Open the format menu. There's font and paragraph. Would that be it?'

'Possibly, but what else is there in that list?'

'Ah! Text direction, and it's got some little vertical arrows next to it. But it's not highlighted so that means I can't use it at the moment.'

'That's right. So how can we get it highlighted, do you think?'

'I don't know. Haven't a clue.'

'OK. Well the fact that it isn't highlighted means that it isn't available to you while you're doing what you are doing now, which is. . ?

'Sorry, you've lost me.'

'Well, at the moment you are writing normal text and we can see that text direction is not available. What else can you do with the word processor? Even if it seems to have nothing to do with text?'

'I'm still not sure what you are getting at. The only other thing you can do with it that I know of is to draw things and I don't want to do that.'

'You're right, but drawing is the key to vertical text with this package. How do you get the drawing toolbar up?'

'That's easy. View. Toolbars. Drawing. Now! Now there's a box with an A in it.'

'Yes, that's a text box. Try that and see what happens to the text direction. Let me know in a few minutes how you get on. And tell me why you think they designed it that way.'

'You always leave me with a question.'

This type of questioning leads learners to discover how to solve their problems without telling them the answers and it provides feedback and encouragement. It leaves them in control rather than having their learning process taken over by the coach. After all it is their learning, not the coach's. They are more likely to remember in the future by reconstructing the thought processes they went through when they worked out their own way to the answer than if they try to recall a 'do this, do that, then that', set of instructions.

Adjust your approach to suit the circumstances. For example, in word processing the basic actions that are used every day can be taught well by the tell-show-do method. But to learn to find the more unusual features of the software the learners need to build an almost instinctive understanding of the package that develops through exploration and reflection. The parting statement by the coach invites the learner to reflect on the design of the package (without using such a frightening phrase) and requires him or her to report progress in a given time-scale (a few minutes). It also provides reassurance that the coach will be back. The learner is not abandoned.

This coaching by questioning (or coaching by exploration or discovery) raises the level of awareness that the individual has of the problem and the possible approaches to solving it, including unproductive routes. It takes little bits of problems, concepts and ideas, and helps the learner to move from conscious incompetence to conscious competence. In this way some additional information that might help to solve future problems is also retained.

Often there is no standard solution or the problem is unique or unusual. Coaching by questions may be the only way forward. The coaching becomes a problem-solving session, with the coach guiding the problem-solving methods but the individual actually solving the problem.

Referring back to the theories of motivation, you will see that the emphasis on your belief that the individual will find a good solution, coupled with the satisfaction and praise he or she gets when successful, are strong motivators. This is a much more powerful approach than tell-show-do and should be preferred whenever possible.

To summarize

Coaching by questions is a learning route that relies heavily on allowing the individuals to discover and learn for themselves how to do things, allowing them to make mistakes and learn from them. Discussion and guidance are provided so as to prevent disasters and gross waste of time. Arguably this is the best system of coaching because what is learned tends to stick.

- ❑ Learning by questions and exploration helps the learning to stick longer.
- ❑ It is more suitable for complex tasks, especially where there is no 'standard' way of doing things.
- ❑ It may be more suitable for senior or experienced staff than for inexperienced ones.
- ❑ The coach asks questions so as to provide guidance on the methods to use but the delegates solve the problems.

Opportunity coaching

Opportunity coaching is simply an attitude of mind on behalf of the manager or coach who always and quite naturally looks for opportunities to help people to learn, and does this by asking questions. It is simple and powerful and uses the Kolb Learning Cycle, described in Chapter 5, as its focus.

For example, when a subordinate reports back on a sales visit the manager listens carefully to the feedback and asks questions, partly to elicit information about the task but also to get the subordinate to question his or her own methods. The manager is using the feedback session to take the subordinate around the Kolb Learning Cycle. Not content with learning the details of what happened (the experience in Kolb's jargon) – which is where many managers stop – the manager uses questions based on the six Ws to prompt the subordinate to reflect on the hows and whys of the experience, to draw conclusions and draft some plans for continuous improvement. These can be tested the next time the individual meets that or any other customer, and the results can be discussed the next time they themselves meet together.

Opportunity coaching is simply instant coaching by questions. It embraces the Kolb Learning Cycle in its entirety. In this way, subordinates generate ideas for improvement as a result of the coaching by questions and they learn to apply the Kolb cycle themselves, so eventually leading to the ultimate aim of self-coaching.

Always watch for opportunities for impromptu coaching

opportunities. If you have not used this technique in the past introduce it gradually, otherwise your staff may feel they are suddenly facing an inquisition. Almost any feedback session when staff are reporting back to you is a good time. Many managers stop after the first stage of the Kolb cycle, content to get the information but missing the opportunity to learn so as to improve. Make a point of using the remaining three stages with your staff by stopping for a moment to reflect with them on what has happened, drawing conclusions and agreeing any changes for similar future situations. Generalise specific learning points so that they can be applied to dissimilar situations as well.

ATTITUDE OF MIND

Skilful coaching depends on an attitude of mind by the coach. If the coach sees the learner as an individual who has talents and gifts, interest and potential, more to offer and the willingness to offer it, then there is the possibility that effective coaching can get started. More than that, recognize that every one of your staff can benefit from coaching, and that you yourself can as well. From the lowest achiever to the highest performer, all can benefit from coaching although as a good manager you also need to look to your other high priorities. Do not start by trying to coach everyone at once.

A successful and vibrant young company appointed a new part-time chairman to the board. He was a semi-retired business executive with long experience of large companies. He saw one of his main functions as coaching members of the board. Every time he met with a director, part of the time was spent on coaching using many very probing questions.

Learning point:
No one is too important to be coached.

Coaches take McGregor's Theory Y approach and picture individuals climbing upwards through Maslow's hierarchy. To help that climb they treat individuals as mature adults who want to do their best and make their contribution (Argyris). They have brought their brains to work with them and want to use them. Even if the tasks are new they can be delegated with necessary, but minimal controls put in place. Individuals are trusted to take responsibility for achieving something they have never done before, under the coach's guidance, and they are delegated the authority to do it. Coaches question what has been achieved and how it was done, how the individual feels and why, and what they have learned. The individuals are like seeds that can be watered and nurtured to grow. Eventually they will go on to water and nurture other seeds who, in their turn, will repeat the process. What you start now will be ongoing.

On the other hand, if managers merely see individuals as people they have to use because of the pressures they themselves are under, and they believe this is bound to produce problems, then problems there will be. Subordinates will be watched every step of the way and managers will take over at tricky parts, and when things go wrong.

In extreme cases such managers take McGregor's Theory X approach and see no one but themselves climbing Maslow's hierarchy. They treat individuals as children but would be astonished if anyone said so. Staff may want to help but they are not yet capable, although there may be bits that they can do if they are watched carefully. Such managers build no esteem and in fact they take it away without realizing it. Even if someone has done the task before, this time it is too important or urgent to leave it to him or her. If it is delegated and it goes wrong then their own manager must share the blame for forcing them to delegate more. Already in their minds they are allocating blame for a task that has not even begun.

They will impose too many controls, keep responsibility to themselves and see this as sensible management. They will interrogate individuals about what has been achieved and who has complained. They will probably achieve the tasks in the end, often by dumping, and the individuals may have learned something but not as much as could have been learned. At the end these managers will probably feel satisfied, they have done their best with the staff available. They might even congratulate the individuals. Self-esteem may have been raised a little but the staff may feel that they could have done much more. They are still like seeds, but seeds that are in danger of being slowly ground into flour.

The latter view is an extreme one but we have all seen managers inadvertently aspire to it. Refusing to let go, being told to delegate more, feeling that 'I can do it better myself'; all are signs of an attitude of mind that is not conducive to coaching.

If, as a manager, you can open your eyes to the potential in others, opening their eyes wider as well, then you are on your way to being a good coach and a better manager and to achieving more, through your team, than you ever thought possible. As you get better at coaching you will instinctively come to use coaching by questions more and more.

We need to strive to improve our ability at this questioning style of coaching and management because for many of us it is not an instinctive approach. In the hierarchy of learning terms we need to progress through the boxes, moving from conscious incompetence through conscious competence until eventually we achieve unconscious competence at coaching by questions. To achieve this put the emphasis on:

Explaining why	more than	Telling what
Listening	more than	Talking
Watching	more than	Doing
Questioning	more than	Answering
Guiding	more than	Controlling
Prompting	more than	Solving
Praising	more than	Criticizing
Suggesting	more than	Telling.

And giving feedback which is specific, positive, and clear.

SUMMARY

Examine the styles you use when you coach and try to use the coaching by questions approach as much as possible. When you receive feedback from your staff do not be content to use only step one of the Kolb Learning Cycle. Use coaching by questions to encourage yourself and others to strive for continual improvement. Test your attitude towards your staff and develop the Theory Y approach.

8

COACHING – A PROCESS

Many people have tried to break coaching down into a step-by-step process, and with some success. Having a step-by-step process is helpful in many ways although it presents some problems as well.

The step-by-step process can only be a guide and not a prescriptive formula. You will always start at the beginning and finish at the end, but you will not always progress in an orderly sequence through intervening steps. Sometimes, perhaps most times, you will progress by leaping back and forth between stages. Coaching is like that.

As we have seen, the coaching process must be integrated into the delegation and so what is described here must be integrated into the delegation process described in Chapter 4.

When shown diagrammatically the coaching process appears far more complicated than it actually is. In some cases the entire process can be completed very quickly. The example in the last chapter about using vertical text in a word processor would have lasted just a few minutes. In other cases, with long and complex tasks, it can take weeks. It all depends on the task, the individual and you.

BEFORE, DURING AND AFTER

Before

Spot the opportunity

There is a continuum between the two extremes of looking for a person to do an existing task and looking for a task to develop a

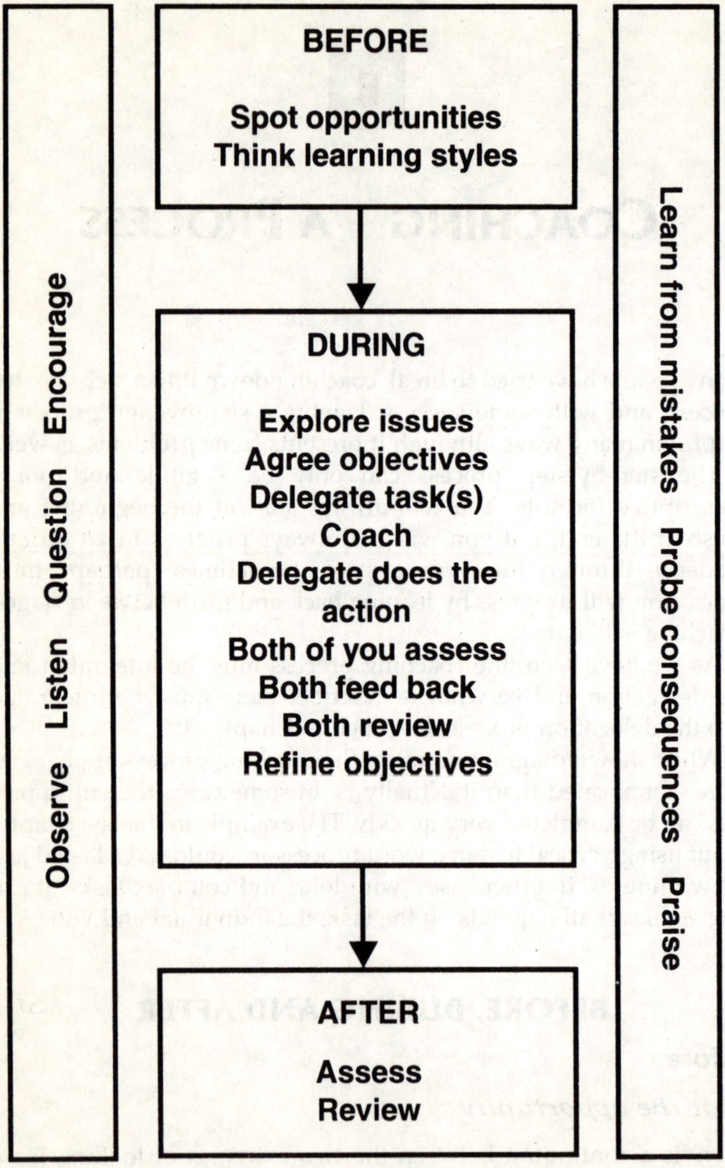

Figure 8.1 *A process for coaching*

person. But there is also a third way: that you spot someone doing something that could be done better, what earlier we called opportunity coaching.

Think learning styles

Try to incorporate all four learning styles into your coaching but take particular account of the individual's preferred learning styles. In non-urgent cases encourage him or her to use other styles as well. For example, encourage an activist to slow down and reflect more.

During

Explore the issues

Talk with people, not at them. Explain what you intend to do and get their reaction. Are they fearful, scared of failing? Discuss the objectives. Reassure them that they are not on their own. Agree levels of responsibility, accountability and authority, stop points and when and how coaching will take place. Ensure that this is a genuine two-way communication, not a monologue from you. Listen to their concerns.

Agree the objectives

Agree the delegated task and the objectives. Unlike delegation, you now need two sets of objectives:

1. Objectives relating to the task.
2. Objectives relating to what you want them to learn.

Clearly differentiate between the two objectives and leave them in no doubt that both have to be achieved. Explain in plain language which learning styles you want to help them to improve and make this part of the learning objective. Often it will include reflection. Put both objectives into writing including the deadlines.

Coach

Ask questions to explore the issues. How the coaching takes place depends very much on what the task is. Asking someone to draw up next year's departmental budget for the first time will require a quite different setting and approach to helping someone to improve his or her word processing skills. Question to probe the possible outcomes and consequences of proposed actions and to reveal any flaws.

Action

The individual might now go away to do the task or an agreed part of it, coming back either when help is needed or a stop point has been reached, or the task may be performed as you watch. Whatever happens, the action is that person's.

Review and feedback

Together look back at what has happened since the last meeting. Discuss what has gone well and why, and not so well and why. Make it an unemotional assessment of the facts. Do as much of this as possible by asking for the individual's views, getting him or her to do the analysis led by your questions. Use praise and encouragement and, if it will help, discuss your own previous successes and failures in this area. Do this carefully. Do not turn the review into a monologue about you. Explore what comes next. Coach and authorize progress to the next stop point.

Refine the objectives

If necessary refine the objectives by agreement, bringing them up to date in the light of what has happened so far.

After

Assessment

Be objective about the final assessment, separately judging the outcomes against the agreed objectives for both the task and the learning. If these were defined properly in terms of outcomes and deadlines then both of you should reach the same conclusions. Ideally an assessment should be factual, keeping opinions to a minimum. See the sections on assessment in Chapters 4 and 9.

Final review

Exchange views about successes and failures, what has been learned and which learning styles have been developed. Ask for feedback about your own performance as a coach – you too are learning from this process. You will now want to delegate more, possibly this task on a permanent basis or something else. Ask the delegate to think about what he or she would like next.

In parallel

In parallel with these activities always be ready to observe, listen, question and encourage. Accept mistakes because you also make mistakes but expect both of you to learn from them. When actions are suggested probe the possible consequences, especially if you feel the proposal is unsound. When something good happens, give congratulations or praise. Try to remember how you felt the first time you did this activity or whenever you try any new activity. Your delegate is trying something new, and that can be daunting.

OPPORTUNITIES TO COACH

Coaching opportunities lie in the eye of the beholder. The more coaching you do, the more opportunities you will see. However, there are some occasions that naturally present opportunities for coaching. These include times when:

- ❑ Someone new joins the department.
- ❑ Someone is promoted.
- ❑ New machinery or software arrives.
- ❑ A new system or process has to be devised or implemented.
- ❑ There is a special problem to be solved.
- ❑ A new project or working party starts.
- ❑ The annual budget has to be prepared.
- ❑ Jobs are restructured or rotated.
- ❑ Someone is on sick leave or holiday.
- ❑ Someone is performing below standard.
- ❑ After a training course.

What other times present natural opportunities for coaching in your team or organization? The more you look for them, the more you will find.

COUNSELLING

Strictly, counselling is not coaching. It is a means of helping someone to come to terms with, and perhaps solve, his or her own problems. Managers can get drawn into counselling when they have staff who have attitude, behavioural or personal problems that are affecting the quality of their work.

If managers have developed their coaching skills they may have the potential to counsel staff when the occasion is right because some of the skills are the same. The techniques revolve around listening and questioning, especially listening, to get to the core problem that the individual may actually prefer to avoid. The counsellor should display understanding while remaining objective.

The aim of counselling is to help the other person to help him or herself while keeping all responsibility and accountability with that person. Under no circumstances should a counsellor attempt to solve the problem for the individual. Unlike delegation and coaching, the counsellor bears no responsibility whatsoever for solving the problem and has no authority to do so. You, as the manager, are not delegating any problem to be solved or any task to be achieved. In counselling, the problem or task is the individual's in its entirety.

A second objective of counselling is to help the person to bring out the emotions that are bottled up inside as a result of the problem being faced. In some counselling sessions emotions can break through as intense sobbing, shaking and grief. This can come as a shock to managers and few can cope with that in their office. It can needlessly leave both parties feeling embarrassed unless they are prepared for the possibility.

If you are counselling someone, do it in private where you will not be disturbed. In today's social climate be wary of the opposite sex on your own. The accepted advice is no anyone of the opposite sex unless you have a chaperone o with you. It may sound overly cautious but it is sound advice on the experience of many counsellors.

Finally, if you are not a trained counsellor recognize your ow limitations in this field. Acute personal problems are not for amateur dabbling. If you have any doubts about your own abilities suggest that either you refer the individual to the personnel department (but only with permission) or suggest talking with his or her doctor. The person may be very reluctant to trust someone from the personnel department, perhaps fearing that something will be written into his or her file. Some companies offer a confidential external counselling service to staff.

The main message for the untrained counsellor is that you can get out of your depth very quickly so, if you have any doubts, refer the person to the professionals.

Counselling has several stages, not all of which will be used on every occasion:

- ❑ Talk about the problem. What is it? Ask questions to help the person to understand the situation. Do not be judgmental even if you are shocked by what you hear. Judging will make counselling much harder and it is hard enough as it is.
- ❑ Bring out the emotions. How does the person feel? It is okay to cry and be angry about things. This can make counselling at work very difficult. Be prepared for it and for your own reactions to it. Redundancy counselling can produce intense emotions.
- ❑ Help the person to see the problem from different angles and to see and explore options. Ask questions. Provide assurances of your support without solving the problem.
- ❑ Encourage the person to choose a solution. Make sure he or she is ready for this stage, do not rush it. Help that person to move into planning to put the solution into action.
- ❑ Restore emotions before the end. Turn from listening to summarizing. Use a business-like manner to restore the atmosphere to normal and emotions to stability. Be sure to end with this stage if emotions have been flowing.

Real life will be far more complex than this simple model. Use it as a framework, repeating stages as often as needed. Do not solve problems for people. They have to live with the results, not you.

COACHING THROUGH OTHERS

Sometimes the manager may not be the ideal person to do the coaching. If you have others within your department who can do the coaching for you, consider delegating the task to them. Sometimes you may have to go outside your department to get the specialist help you need. One aspect of an ideal team is that the members coach one another without seeing it as anything special.

Informal learning opportunities

These days there are many informal learning opportunities for those who have the will and the aptitude to use them. For example, those who have a reasonably well-developed theorist learning style can make use of books, training videos, CD ROMS and computer-based training. Activists can experiment if this can be done safely. Pragmatists can interrogate others who already do the task, and reflectors can think things through for themselves and try it out.

ACTION

Who will you coach? Refer back to the exercise at the end of Chapter 4 where you picked your top three combinations of people and tasks. Think about these people and decide which two learning styles they each seem to prefer and how this should influence your approach. Check Table 7.1 and decide which method could be used to coach them most successfully. Then turn to the before-during-after process and decide how to start. Use the delegation and coaching planning sheet at the end of this chapter as a guide, it is a development of that provided at the end of Chapter 4. Design your own to suit your circumstances. Check the delegation process described in Chapter 4 as you will need that also, and get to work.

SUMMARY

While coaching is an attitude of mind it is useful to build your actions around a model process which requires you to do things before, during and after the delegated task is performed. Learn to recognize natural opportunities to coach people, consider their natural learning style and agree objectives for both the task and the learning. Coach by asking questions about what they might do and why, not by telling them what to do. Recognize situations that need professional rather than amateur counselling, and if you do offer counselling never solve the problem for them.

DELEGATION AND COACHING PLANNING SHEET

Define the task: *Outcomes/results required, standards to be achieved.*

Deadlines, time-scales:

The person:

Reason why: *Relation to departmental or company goals and business plan.*

Resources needed: *Manpower, environment, material, money, information, machines.*

Training needed: *Courses, coaching, books, tapes, visit to expert, learning packages.*

Level of authority delegated:

Level 1:	*Look into it.*		
Level 2:	*Suggest alternatives.*		
Level 3:	*Make recommendations.*		
Level 4:	*Start after I approve.*	*Proceed to stop point.*	*Approval first.*
Level 5:	*Start before I approve.*	*Proceed to stop point.*	*Act and report.*
Level 6:	*Do it all.*	*Tell me later.*	*Full authority.*

Known stop points:

Monitoring: *Methods, frequency, meetings. Effectiveness and efficiency.*

Other people to tell:

Top two learning styles: Activist Reflector Theorist Pragmatist
How will you use these styles?

Coaching method: tell-show-do ________ coaching by questions

What is likely to be their reaction?

How will you deal with it?

9

TECHNIQUES

In this chapter we look at some of the techniques you will need when delegating and coaching. You will definitely need the skills of questioning, listening, observing, setting objectives, interviewing and giving feedback. You will also need many of the attitudes described, especially respect for others. The other techniques you will need often, but maybe not on every occasion. Read about each one and question your own present skill. A suggestion is made at the end to help you to identify which ones to try to strengthen.

QUESTIONING

Asking questions and listening to the answers are the keys to coaching. The purpose of the questions is to help you as coach to steer the conversation so that the individual is drawn into considering situations, problems, facts, opinions, feelings, emotions and so on that might not have been considered otherwise. Or to consider them in a wider and deeper way so as to clarify the situation, sort out the individual's own thinking and talk about his or her thoughts and expectations.

The manner in which you ask your questions and the motive that lies behind them are crucial in determining success. If you are seen by the individual as caring and concerned, and interested in him or her as well as the task, then your chances of success are increased.

A good process to follow is:

- ❑ Focus on the problem or situation rather than on the solution.

- ❑ Probe the individual's understanding and open up matters not previously considered.
- ❑ Ask for his or her ideas for solutions.
- ❑ Explore the consequences of putting his or her suggestions into action, especially if you consider the suggestions to be inappropriate.
- ❑ Encourage the person to select his or her own course of action.

When you are planning your meeting think of the topics you want to cover and write down some opening questions for each topic that will get the other person talking. Also identify any specific points you want to know about. Other than that, let the answers lead you to areas to probe in depth.

There are many categories of questions, the two basic ones being called open and closed. Together with probing questions they are the three types that you ought to use most. There are others that should be avoided in most circumstances, although some do have positive uses.

Do you really need to know about categories of questions? As an academic exercise, probably not; if they are potentially helpful, then probably yes. In fact they are helpful and they are not complicated. You can use them very easily to help you when phrasing questions and so increase your chances of success.

Open questions are used to get the other person talking, probing questions to dig deeper into a subject, and closed questions to get definitive answers especially 'yes' or 'no'. They are sometimes pictured as a mental funnel to channel the other person to the core of the problem.

Open questions

Open questions are open-ended and they help to open up a discussion. They invite the other person to do the talking, so use them at the start of a conversation or new topic or whenever you want that person to take the lead. They give the other person space, an open playing field on which to operate, and so they help to build rapport and show you are interested in what that person thinks. Because they invite the other person to do the talking they can help to put people at their ease.

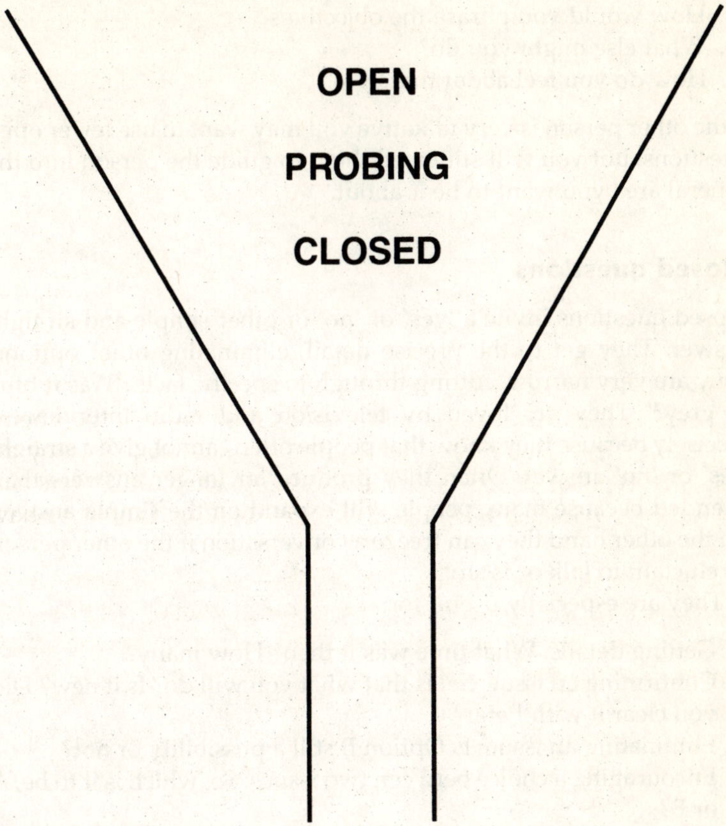

Figure 9.1 *Using questions to funnel down to detail*

1. Tell me about the situation.
2. How are things?
3. How did you go about it?
4. What happened?
5. What do you propose to do?
6. So what will you do next?
7. Give me an example.
8. What should the outcomes be?

9. How would you phrase the objectives?
10. What else might you do?
11. How do you feel about that?

If the other person is very talkative you may want to use fewer open questions, but you will still need them to guide the person into the general area you want to hear about.

Closed questions

Closed questions invite a 'yes' or 'no' or other simple and straight answer. They get to the precise detail, eliminating other options. They are very narrow, cutting through to specific facts. 'Was it blue or grey?' They are loved by television and radio interviewers precisely because they know that people often cannot give a straight 'yes' or 'no' answer. Often they produce far longer answers than intended because many people will expand on the simple answer. On the other hand they can freeze a conversation if the other person is reluctant to talk or is shy.

They are especially useful for:

- ❑ Getting details: What time was it then? How many?
- ❑ Confirming an issue: So, is that what you will do? Is it new? Did you clear it with Peter?
- ❑ Eliminating an issue: Is Option B still a possibility or not?
- ❑ Encouraging a choice between two issues: So, which is it to be, A or B?
- ❑ Pushing the individual to examine some additional details they were skimming over: Are you sure about that? Did he say will or might? Was there any room for doubt?

But avoid closed questions if you want a lot of information:

- ❑ Have you thought about...? (Yes).
- ❑ Did you try...? (No).
- ❑ Would it be a good idea to...? (Don't know).

Probing questions

Probing questions follow on from open questions and are used to dig deeper. They focus in more, either to bring out the detail or to set the other person off down a different track. You will also use probing questions when you are not willing to accept what has been said at face value, when you believe there is more to be known. They can be open or closed and they are likely to be the ones you use most often.

- ❑ You mentioned several things including the budget. Is there a problem with the budget?
- ❑ When will that problem be resolved?
- ❑ Tell me about what you can do to help resolve it.
- ❑ Of the other points you made, which is the most important?
- ❑ Did he definitely rule it out, or is there still a chance?
- ❑ OK, I understand that. What happened next?
- ❑ You said a few. How many?
- ❑ Tell me more about the delivery problems.

Those are the three basic categories of questions and generally they are the best ones to use. Practice identifying the sort of questions you use and when you use them. Start deliberately using specific categories in specific situations. Start with open questions to encourage them to talk and bring out the issues. Dig into issues with probing questions and establish the precise facts with closed questions.

Hypothetical questions

Hypothetical questions bring hypothetical answers and normally you should avoid them, especially during assessments. However, if used carefully in a coaching situation they can play a valuable role in encouraging reflection.

Once you have a good understanding of the situation the individual has been in and what action was taken, it might be useful to explore alternative actions that could have been taken. Either these were rejected at the time or were never thought of. Hypothetical questions, if asked wisely and pursued by probing questions, can take the individual down an alternative route to the one actually taken – at least in thought. It is what Einstein called a thought experiment.

Good hypothetical questions can encourage reflection:

- ❑ What would you do differently next time?
- ❑ What might have happened if you had chosen the alternative route?
- ❑ Let's think that one through. Suppose you do that. What might be the consequences for Department X?

Too often hypothetical questions are asked out of laziness because the questioner is not focusing on the reality of what is happening or has happened. If you are not focused on the reality, you cannot coach.

Leading questions – avoid

Leading questions are those that suggest, or hint at, the answer you want to hear and invite the other person to agree with you. Again radio and television interviewers seem to be fond of them and use them as challenges. Generally they are best avoided. Even if you are sure of your ground and want to lead the conversation to a close there are better ways than a leading question. Instead, use a short summary and ask a closed question. 'So, we're agreed that you accept this delegated task with these time constraints. Is that right?'

Avoid leading questions that begin:

- ❑ Don't you think that...
- ❑ I suppose you will...
- ❑ Wouldn't you agree that...
- ❑ Don't you feel that...

Multiple questions – avoid

Multiple questions contain several questions rolled into one. The questions are usually related to one another and get bunched together because of over-enthusiasm or nervousness on the part of the questioner. Normally the listener can only remember the last question in the list and replies to that, or gets confused.

- ❑ Do you really think they will agree to a contract like that or are you going to make concessions? Timing might be important or is it, or do you think they'll just go for the discount?

Always avoid multiple questions. It is better to split them up and ask them separately.

Judgemental questions – avoid

These are questions that imply a judgement, usually a negative one, about the action taken by the other person. Parents are good at these. Often they are closed questions and the tone of voice will usually reinforce the negative view of the questioner. Never use them in coaching. If there is something to criticize use your questions to bring the other person to the point where he or she can see the error. Remember that you have joint responsibility in this delegation and coaching business.

- ❑ Surely you didn't say you couldn't do it?
- ❑ You still haven't checked it?
- ❑ Do you realize how much that costs?
- ❑ How could anyone possibly think that was a good idea?

Additional techniques for eliciting information

You already use several other techniques for drawing out more information from people without actually asking specific questions:

Silence

Silence allows the other person to think quietly during the conversation. Too often people rush in to fill a silence, perhaps through feeling embarrassed if nothing is seen to be happening. Occasionally allow silences to linger. Let the other person break the silence. If he or she has said something and stopped, it can be a good idea to wait to see if more will be added. If you keep quiet, the other person may pick up the subject again.

Paraphrasing

An excellent technique for confirming your understanding. Paraphrasing means repeating back to the other person the gist of what he or she has said but in your words. It invites that person to confirm or add further information. 'So what you are saying is. . .'

Body language

You probably use simple body language quite naturally such as a raised eyebrow, a nod, a shake of the head, shrugs or other movements to signal an unspoken question, agreement or disagreement.

Exclamations

'Go on!' 'He said that?' Simple words or phrases can encourage further outpourings.

Repeating key words

This confirms that you are listening and asks for confirmation or explanation and is especially useful if the other person is exaggerating. 'Refused?' 'Thirty thousand?' 'Always?' 'Never?'

Action

What types of questions do you need to use more of and less of? How will you bring about the change?

Listen to radio and television interviewers. Spot the different types of questions they use and ask yourself why they use them.

LISTENING

The phrase 'active listening' has crept into management jargon. It is a good phrase though, because listening is not the passive action it is often thought to be. Good listening requires active participation by the listener. It is genuinely hard work because it requires continuous concentration: thinking, questioning and checking that your understanding is correct.

Listening is almost the tail-end of the communication process and is usually performed the worst, perhaps because it apparently requires no effort. Think of communication as a process for getting information from one brain to another. It has four parts:

1. Sorting the information in the speaker's brain.
2. Saying it clearly, in the right language, at the right speed, with the right tone, pitch and volume.
3. Listening, receiving the information accurately and picking up any nuances and tone.
4. Sorting and understanding it in the listener's brain, including the difficult bits and the hidden meanings.

Failure to communicate in one-to-one situations is not usually because of speech impediments or hearing difficulties but more often because of poor effort by the listener. Listening is far more than hearing.

Our brains work far faster than anyone can talk, so our thoughts may drift as we listen or we continue doing something else while reassuring the speaker with phrases like, 'Go on, I'm listening.' Clearly we say things like that because of some indication from the speaker that he or she thinks we are not listening properly. Perhaps we are ignoring much of what is being said, just picking out the parts that interest us, or maybe we hear it all but do not relate to it. It is comparatively rare that we take it all in, understand it, pick up the feelings of the person and genuinely relate to that person and situation. But that is what is needed if you are going to coach well, at least on anything complicated.

At its best listening involves:

- ❑ Hearing.
- ❑ Understanding the information.
- ❑ Understanding the emotions.
- ❑ Checking your understanding.
- ❑ Seeing it from the person's viewpoint, without necessarily agreeing.

Stephen Covey has suggested that most of the time most of us listen at one of four levels (Covey, 1992):

1. Ignoring: Hearing but not really listening at all.
2. Pretending: Hearing and making encouraging responses, 'Yes. Uh-huh. Right.'
3. Selective listening: Listening only to parts.
4. Attentive listening: Paying attention and focusing energy on the words that are being said.

But Covey suggests there is a fifth level which most of us do not use often enough:

5. Empathic listening (from empathy): listening with intent to understand, emotionally and intellectually. Getting inside the person's frame of reference.

You will not achieve any coaching if you use only the first two levels. You might achieve some by chance at level three. You will achieve more using level four, but level five is where you really need to be.

> **As a measure of how well you have listened and understood someone, to what extent do you understand his or her unspoken motivations?**

So how can you know how good you are at listening? The following points include many learned from trainers who help managers to improve their listening skills. How many of the good points and how many of the poor points apply to you?

Good points: you are listening when

1. You really try to understand even when the speaker is confused.
2. You summarize accurately in your own words what the speaker has struggled to say.
3. With just an occasional word you encourage the speaker to keep going.
4. You grasp the speaker's point of view even when it's against your own beliefs.

5. You restrain your rush to give advice.
6. You encourage the speaker to work out what is really going on.
7. You allow the speaker the peace of silence without hurrying him or her on.
8. The speaker tells you things at a deeper level than originally intended.
9. Your questions go to the heart of the matter.
10. The speaker feels better or more confident afterwards.

Poor points: you are not listening when

1. You say you understand before the speaker has finished talking.
2. You finish the speaker's sentences.
3. You tell the speaker about your own similar experiences instead of listening to his or hers.
4. You answer the speaker's problem before he or she has finished stating it.
5. You are aching to tell the speaker about something else.
6. You completely misunderstand the speaker's feelings on the matter.
7. You talk to someone else at the same time.
8. You do something demanding at the same time, such as reading or writing.
9. You feel you have to tell the speaker that you are listening.
10. Your questions do not help.

How did you score? Did you score more on the good points than the poor ones, or was it the other way round?

Many techniques have been suggested to help people to become better at listening. Some of the popular ideas are listed below. These ideas are genuinely useful but built into them is a potential problem. Use and practise the techniques to improve your listening skills by all means, but do not let the techniques become goals in themselves. It is possible to use the techniques as a display without improving your listening one iota. The best method is not a technique at all. It is simply having a genuine interest in the person and what he or she is saying.

The techniques of active listening

- ❑ Repeat key words as an encouragement and confirmation that you have heard and understood.
- ❑ Paraphrase: Briefly play back what has been said but in your own words. This will confirm that you are listening and will check your understanding.
- ❑ Summarize the main points and any decisions taken at the end of a topic. This is more than paraphrasing as you are providing a summary of a section.
- ❑ Have a relaxed body posture. Lean forward slightly but do not invade the speaker's personal space. Use nods and smiles to signal encouragement or agreement.
- ❑ Use the right amount of eye contact. Staring is threatening. Move your point of focus around between the eyes and the bridge of the nose. Avoiding eye contact suggests you are uninterested.
- ❑ Silence: Allow the speaker time to think. Let him or her end the silences most times. This also prevents you from rushing in with inappropriate reactions just to fill the silence.
- ❑ Listen to the tone and how things are said, not just what is said. The tone will often tell you about feelings as well as facts.
- ❑ Reflect the speaker's feelings. 'You felt annoyed.' Show that you understand the speaker's feelings without necessarily agreeing with them.
- ❑ Stop the speaker when you lose the thread of the argument or do not understand. Ask for clarification.
- ❑ Use simple phrases to encourage. 'Go on,' 'And then what?'

Suggested actions

During and after listening to someone ask yourself three simple questions. If you can answer them accurately and in detail you have been listening well.

1. What are the facts of the matter?
2. How does the speaker feel about them?
3. What is the speaker going to do about them?

On a scale of one (poor) to five (excellent), how do you think the following people would rate you as a listener:

- ❑ Your manager.
- ❑ Your subordinates.
- ❑ Other colleagues.
- ❑ Your spouse or partner.
- ❑ Your parents or children.

Later, try asking them.

OBSERVING

The third key to coaching, along with questioning and listening, is observing. You may need to observe in two different situations. First when you are watching tasks being performed in front of you, and secondly when individuals are reporting back to you on what they have done. In the first case you will probably be observing to note their skill and their confidence; in the latter case you will be observing their body language to fill in the gaps left by what they tell you.

The key to observing is to know what you are looking for. There could be at least three things: the outcome, the process that led to it and the behaviour of the people as they perform the process or report to you. If you can define what good performance looks like in these terms then you will have done much of your preparation for your observation of the people concerned.

- ❑ Observe the outcome.
- ❑ Observe the process.
- ❑ Observe the behaviour.

In the last few years many organizations have defined what good performance looks like for a whole range of their activities. These definitions are usually called competencies and in some cases they define poor performance, good performance and superior performance. Many trades and professions also have detailed definitions of levels of performance in their National Vocational Qualification (NVQ) frameworks. Use them if they are appropriate.

They may give you a lot of guidance in terms of outcomes, processes and behaviours.

More usually you will provide your own measures. The outcomes are already defined in the tasks and learning objectives. The process is usually at the discretion of the delegate and you may not see it all, although you will monitor it and the delegate will talk you through it. You may also consider asking other people who may have witnessed it, if that is appropriate.

Observing behaviour

It is easier to observe behaviour than to make objective judgements about attitude or personality. With behaviour you can concentrate on facts alone, with attitude or personality it is simply your opinion against theirs and an open invitation to an argument.

In delegation and coaching you are usually judging whether the individuals look confident and at ease with what is happening (whether doing the task or talking with you) or look uncomfortable, nervous and hesitant. If the latter, is it simply because you are observing them or because they are unsure of what they are doing?

It has been said that up to half of personal communication is by body language. Most of what we as amateurs have learned about body language has been assimilated over the years without conscious effort. We have learned to 'read' people. For the non-expert, trying to be clever at reading body language can lead to silliness, so just try these simple questions and any of your own that are relevant:

- ❑ Do they look sure of themselves or unsure?
- ❑ Are their actions hesitant or confident?
- ❑ Do they look comfortable or uncomfortable?
- ❑ Do they perform their actions skilfully or awkwardly?
- ❑ Do they meet or avoid eye contact?
- ❑ Do they seem agitated or calm?
- ❑ Are they smiling or frowning?
- ❑ Is their speech hurried, quiet and stumbling, or is it strong and calm?
- ❑ Is their tone of voice friendly and confident, or abrupt and challenging?

Finally, be wary of your own prejudices towards their mannerisms. We all have prejudices and we all have mannerisms. You may simply not like some of their mannerisms but that does not mean that the delegated task is not being achieved or that they are not learning from your coaching.

AGREEING OBJECTIVES

In delegation and coaching you need to have a mutual understanding of what has to be achieved. The terminology can be confusing. Are we talking about aims, goals, results, outcomes or objectives? Does it matter which word we use? Because many people use these terms loosely while others operate a rigorous hierarchy it is better if you agree with the individual just what you mean. Whatever word you use make it cover three things:

- ❑ The task: what has to be done.
- ❑ The standard: how well it has to be done.
- ❑ The deadline: when it must be completed.

People spend hours trying to write objectives for their staff and that can only mean that something has gone wrong. Some people even claim that there are jobs for which objectives cannot be written, which is nonsense. The basic rules for writing an objective are:

- ❑ Include the three elements: task, standard and deadline.
- ❑ Keep it simple.
- ❑ Get on with it.

Both parties should have a written copy that should be reviewed and updated if circumstances change.

Two of the most common causes of confusion are complexity and measurement.

A complex objective should be treated as a project and broken down into its various tasks, steps or stages. Depending on the ability of the delegate, one or more tasks can be delegated, while being integrated into the whole, or the whole can be delegated as a single unit.

Managers are often advised to make objectives measurable. This confuses people because the word 'measure' can mean a very precise process to some people, such as engineers, scientists and doctors, while to others it means little more than a personal judgement. Measurable simply means having an outcome defined in such a way that there can be no reasonable doubt as to whether or not it has been achieved. This should allow both parties to use their professional judgement, otherwise you end up with unwieldy definitions through attempting something that a lay person can understand. What is the point if lay people are not involved? If the two people involved can understand it you are unlikely to need more.

Finally, a manager can impose an objective by the nature of his or her authority, but it is not normally a good way of managing. The individual's motivation will automatically be higher if he or she has willingly agreed to an objective, or even proposed it, than if you impose it by might. It is good practise to ask the individual to phrase the objective whenever you can.

A commonly used acronym to help when writing objectives is SMART. It stands for:

- ❑ Specific — the task and standard;
- ❑ Measurable — a common-sense way of knowing if the standard has been achieved;
- ❑ Agreed — not imposed;
- ❑ Realistic — it can be done with the time and resources available;
- ❑ Timed — deadlines for reviews, feedback and completion.

In delegation and coaching you are stretching people beyond their present experience. You can expect some resistance or reluctance in the face of this challenge. Help them to face it by providing consistency through clear objectives, changing them only if circumstances dictate, giving your active support and encouragement, and by using the processes for delegation and coaching we have described.

INTERVIEWING

You may not think of a business meeting to delegate or coach as an interview. In this context 'interview' simply means a meeting, probably informal, between the two of you to discuss matters relating to the delegated task or to the coaching. The purpose could be to introduce the idea of delegating a task to the individual, to discuss and agree the objectives, to review progress, or to finalize the assessment and evaluation at the end. It should be informal but not casual.

Preparation

Devote some time to preparing for the meeting. Being unprepared invites disaster. Be clear as to what your own objectives are:

- ❑ To save you time by delegating and to develop them through learning a new skill.
- ❑ Items from your delegation and coaching planning sheet.
- ❑ Your objectives for this meeting. What do you want to achieve in the next 30 minutes?

Think about these other issues:

- ❑ What is likely to be the person's reaction to what you have to say?
- ❑ What objections are likely to be expressed and how will you deal with them?
- ❑ What has been achieved so far?
- ❑ Remind yourself about the accountability, responsibility and the authority you have delegated or intend to delegate.
- ❑ Have you done what you agreed to do at the last meeting?
- ❑ How often do you want the person to report back from now on?
- ❑ What feedback do you want to give, facts and feelings?

Also think about the assumptions you made when you chose this person for this task, assumptions about his or her personality and work. These assumptions should be checked. Things like:

- ❑ She will love this.
- ❑ He will find ways to make the time needed.
- ❑ Of course she can use a spreadsheet.

- ❑ It will need some time away from home but his family will not mind that.
- ❑ She is ambitious and will see this as an opportunity.
- ❑ There will be some stress involved but he's got nothing else to worry about.

Place and time

- ❑ However difficult, try to hold the meeting in a quiet room without interruptions, including telephone interruptions.
- ❑ Allow sufficient time for the meeting and tell the other person how much time you have allowed.

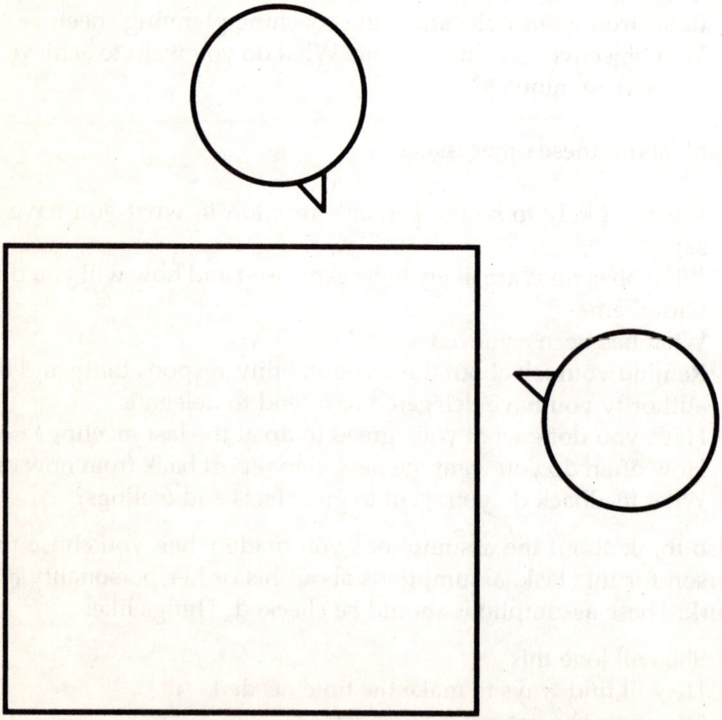

Figure 9.2 *Meet across the corner of the desk*

- ❑ Arrange the chairs in a 'friendly' fashion across a corner of the table, rather than in 'confrontational' style across the table.
- ❑ Make it welcoming and relaxed. Have coffee or tea available, if feasible.

End

- ❑ Summarize the meeting at the end.
- ❑ Confirm the action plan.
- ❑ Get the delegate to write down the next objective, with deadline and any stop point.

NEGOTIATING

There will be many times when you will negotiate with your delegate. Negotiating is about trading and you learned to do it naturally as a child, 'If I eat my cabbage can I have some ice cream?' Now the trade is likely to be more like, 'If I do that for you will you be able to finish a week earlier?'

If you are negotiating you should try to avoid giving things away for free. See if there is something you want in return. Of course, if you have got something seriously wrong listen and learn from your staff and put it right. Later if they want to change things, see if you feel you should give it or trade it.

There are four main stages to negotiations (Kennedy, Benson and McMillan, 1980). They are preparation (as so often), discussion, proposal and bargain.

Preparation

Preparing for negotiation is part and parcel of the preparation you have already made for the delegation and coaching. It will not add much to what is needed there. You already have your objectives for the task and the learning, and there is information to give and receive. All you need to do now is to think of the concessions you could trade if, and only if, it is necessary. You will not need many concessions and they should be small, easy for you to trade but meaningful to your delegate. Remember that they are not gifts to be handed out, they are tokens to trade for other things, including agreement. You might think of things like:

- ❑ I will speak to (difficult person) if you will…
- ❑ I will try to get (better equipment) if you will…
- ❑ I will relieve you of (existing task) if you do this delegated task.
- ❑ I will postpone the deadline on (Task X) if you will…

These, and many more, are the 'ice creams' in your freezer.

Discussion

The purpose of the discussion is for you both to exchange understanding. Explain what you want to do and how you want to do it. Ask for reactions and listen to them carefully. Address any concerns. Ask any questions you have prepared, especially those that test your assumptions. Remember that a discussion is a two-way process, not your monologue. What is the person's reaction, especially his or her feelings?

Proposal

Once the person understands your position and vice versa, either of which may have been modified in the discussion, formally propose the delegated task and the coaching to go with it, and ask for agreement. It is very tempting to immediately try to persuade the individual what a truly great idea this is. It is better to make your proposal and invite a response. Keep quiet and listen. The time for persuasion may come after you have the reaction, not before. In delegation and coaching your proposal should eventually turn into the objectives for the task and learning.

Bargain

This is when you do any bartering or trading, if it is needed. Your aim should be to make only minor adjustments to the deal so that both parties agree and commit themselves to it. It is not a time for major changes. A good manager looks for the win-win-win situation for the delegate, manager and the organization. The final agreement, probably phrased as objectives, should be written down, with copies for both of you. Include the date and time of the first review.

PERSUADING

Persuading is like selling. You need a thorough understanding of what you are actually offering, both the positive and negative aspects. In sales jargon these are the features of your 'product'. You also need to understand the needs and feelings of the delegate. Why would he or she want or not want to take on this delegated task? What is in it for the delegate?

Discuss these in the light of the positive and negative aspects of the task you are proposing. There is no point in avoiding the negative aspects, and there will probably be some. Sooner or later the individual will see them and will know that you avoided talking about them. That is hardly likely to engender trust.

Persuasion is about explaining the benefits, really getting the delegate to see and understand them. Ask about any doubts and problems he or she can foresee. Address these honestly. Help the delegate to see that the positives outweigh the negatives. Use open and probing questions to bring the issues out into the open. Use a closed question to test to see if you are near to agreement, 'If I can satisfy you on that question, do we have an agreement?' (Yes or no.)

REWARDING

How people are rewarded for their efforts and successes will depend on the culture within the company. Of course there are promotions, pay rises and bonuses, but here we are thinking of the simple rewards that managers can give to their staff. Some of these are financial, others not. Even with the financial ones the gain is usually out of all proportion to the cost.

Praise

Praise has been stressed throughout this book. Genuine praise is one of the best rewards you can give to your staff. It bolsters confidence and assures them that you are aware of their efforts and successes. Take advantage of opportunities to give genuine praise to your staff, but be wary of devaluing it by giving it when it is not due or giving it so often that it becomes part of the scenery. Praise can be given:

- ❑ Privately, just between the two of you.
- ❑ Publicly, in front of the team at a team meeting.
- ❑ In writing, and copied to your own manager.
- ❑ By award: some organizations have Staff-of-the-Month awards and similar badges or noticeboard announcements.

Gratitude

A simple thank you or other expression of gratitude when they have genuinely put themselves out is appreciated by all. It builds confidence and self-esteem and assures them that you know what is going on.

Gifts

Many managers are authorized to use their budget to make small gifts of appreciation to staff, not usually cash. Sometimes these are given as gift tokens, tickets for the theatre or a sporting event, bottles of spirits or wine, and so on.

Meals out

One of the most popular, and in many companies the easiest to arrange, is to suggest that the individual takes his or her partner out for a meal and claims the expense, including baby-sitter and taxis, on a company expense claim which you will authorize. Sometimes this can be done even in organizations where there are no 'official' ways of giving small rewards to staff. Be sure to inform your own manager of what you are doing.

Promotional gifts

Many companies give small promotional gifts to customers, such as pens, calculators, mugs, mouse mats, and sometimes more exotic items; all with the company name and logo on the side. Sometimes staff appreciate these little gifts as a thank you.

Time off

For many people a day or a half-day of extra leave with pay is greatly appreciated as a reward for special achievement.

In all these cases the cost to the company is tiny compared to the benefits gained by showing staff that you both care about and appreciate what they have done. The only precaution you need to take in most cases with financial rewards is to check with your own manager and with your management accountant that neither you nor the individual are going to encounter problems, such as company policies or taxation difficulties.

ATTITUDES

Your attitudes are revealed by your behaviour and many positive attitudes are required if you are to be successful at delegation and coaching.

Respect

Value your people for what they are. They are unique individuals who have their own feelings, loves, fears, apprehensions, joys and idiosyncrasies. Respect them as people. Separate their actions from their personality. Acknowledge that they have a right to their own views, while maintaining your role as leader, and that they have the right to make the occasional mistake, just as you do. In a way, when delegating and coaching, see yourself as their helper. They are helping you by taking on this task, now your role is to help them to succeed at it.

Trust

They have to learn by your words and actions that they can trust you. You have to earn their trust; you cannot demand it. If you say you will do something, do it. If you criticize their actions do so in private and base it entirely on the facts you have observed.

Sincerity

The feelings and respect you display must be genuine, not faked or put on for show or to impress. Too many people in business act a part. They may be insincere and most of those around them know it. The pity is that they themselves can be taken in by their own deception.

Enthusiasm

Enthusiasm is infectious. If you show your own enthusiasm for this delegation and coaching then people are more likely to respond than if you appear unconvinced yourself. Your body language, your tone of voice and your words reveal your enthusiasm.

Assertiveness

Being assertive means being neither aggressive nor passive in the way you put things forward. You do not override other people but you repeat your own view until it has registered with them. Treat them as equals in terms of listening to and respecting their views then, provided you have not changed your mind, restate your own views with further explanation and seek acceptance or compromise. If necessary agree to disagree, then ask them to follow your instructions as manager.

Empathy

Empathy is seeing things from their viewpoint and letting them know. This requires considerable sensitivity to, as the dictionary puts it, 'fully comprehend' what they are feeling. It is not quite the same as sympathy, which implies compassion and sharing their feelings and feeling sorry for them. Empathy is trying to see the situation through their eyes, heart and mind.

Interest

Your staff will feel it if you have a genuine interest in them. If you see them as unique individuals, each with something different to contribute, each with some unusual insight or spark of creativity to add to your own, then you will start to show your interest in them as the individuals who together form your team.

Patience

There will be many times when your patience will be tested. If you have delegated a task and you are coaching someone through it for their first time, inevitably you will be able to do things better and quicker much of the time. Remind yourself that an investment of your time now will be paid back many times in the future.

Generosity

Time is a resource you will always be short of. Nevertheless, be generous with your time when delegating and coaching. Without your time now more of your time will be needed later, representing an altogether bigger loss. Spend time listening, questioning, observing, explaining, empathizing and encouraging.

FEEDBACK

Feedback is the process of presenting to individuals your observations and understanding of what they have done, how they did it and what they have achieved. It focuses on the issues and the facts, not on the people concerned. It is part of the whole delegation and coaching process. In feedback you have moved from the central process of coaching, which is questioning, to telling. Even with this it is good practice to start by asking them for their views.

Objective

The objective of feedback is to help them to improve their performance, either by confirming good practice or by pointing out, in a friendly and co-operative manner, areas for improvement along with your evidence and your willingness to help. It is vital that the atmosphere is such that they truly believe that your objective is to help. Otherwise you can easily find yourself in a situation where they are defensive and ready to repel boarders.

Your aims should be to:

- ❑ Present your feedback factually.
- ❑ Discuss it with them.
- ❑ Encourage them to decide what to do as a result.
- ❑ Progress right round the Kolb Learning Cycle.
- ❑ Leave them feeling positive about the whole experience.

You can make it more likely that you achieve the right atmosphere by opening and closing with the positive aspects, and by telling them how much you value their contribution and their willingness to have undertaken this delegated task. Such sentiments must be genuine.

Result

If done well, giving feedback will help to build self-esteem and encourage the climb up Maslow's hierarchy of needs. It should be a Theory Y experience. Done badly it achieves precisely the opposite, leaving hurt feelings and damaged relationships. This is why so many managers are reluctant to give critical feedback. However, it is a manager's right to seek improvements in the work of all staff, but it is an employee's right to expect that to be done with understanding and respect.

How

Feedback should be about facts, not opinions. If for some reason you have to express your opinions then stress that is what they are. Generally your facts will be about the results achieved, the methods used, the delegate's behaviour or manner and your feelings.

Ensure that your comments are clear and concise. Use specific examples such as, 'On Tuesday when you. . .' If you have to criticize then be sure to separate personality from actions. Ask for reactions and for ideas about how to improve. Your objective, remember, is to bring about improvements in performance, not to damage and destroy. Express your feelings in the form, 'I felt. . .' rather than, 'You made me feel. . .'

Opening

Open by reminding the delegate of why you are meeting and ask how he or she thinks it has gone. What is his or her opinion of what has happened?

When

The time to give feedback will usually be during one of your periodic review sessions. The delegate will be expecting feedback then. If given at other times, and other occasions may present themselves, check that the place and timing are appropriate. Over the dinner table in the staff canteen with others listening is hardly an appropriate time or place. There may be occasions when giving feedback in front of other people may be appropriate, such as if you are coaching a group of people. However, as a general rule, give feedback in private as soon as possible after the event and at a time when the delegate might reasonably expect it. Avoid times when he or she is focused on something else.

Criticism

Giving negative feedback is much harder than giving positive feedback. Learn from how you felt the last time that you were on the receiving end. Think back to when you last received criticism:

- ❑ Did you feel that you knew neither what was wrong nor what you were expected to do to put it right?
- ❑ Did you feel the meeting was handled badly?
- ❑ Did you feel that you personally had been criticized rather than your actions?

- ❑ Did you feel that your relationship with the other person was damaged?
- ❑ Were you left feeling angry?
- ❑ Did you strongly disagree with some of what was said?
- ❑ Did you feel that the other person did not listen to you?

How can you avoid mistakes like these when you next have to give negative feedback?

ASSESSING

Assessment is about making an objective judgement of the outcomes of the efforts made to complete the task, at interim stages and at the end. The assessment should be made strictly against the criteria agreed in the original statement of the objective and as amended by any subsequent changes. If the objective was well written, and changes were made sensibly and recorded, then assessment should be relatively easy. Both parties ought to be able to draw virtually the same conclusions.

In assessment, opinions and feelings will obviously be present but they should be kept separate from the assessment itself, which is a judgement on outcomes and results alone.

Assessments are about:

- ❑ whether the task was achieved or not;
- ❑ whether the standard was achieved or not. If not, whether it was exceeded or missed and by how much;
- ❑ whether the deadline was met or not. If not, whether it was undercut or exceeded and by how much.

That is the assessment of the task or learning. It may be followed by an assessment of the performance of the individual and this is where subjective elements rush in. Given the circumstances that prevailed, did the task turn out to be harder or easier than expected or about the same? Someone who met the deadline for one task might have had an easy time whereas someone who just missed the deadline for another might have performed heroically. How will you know?

The answer is that you will not know unless you monitor and review progress, and unless you ask the individual what happened. Good questioning technique and observation are your keys to knowing but it is a fact of life that you will never know as much as the individual concerned unless you were with that person all the time.

Assess the facts on the basis of the objectives. Judge the performance on that and the rest of the information you have available.

FEELINGS

Within our culture feelings come second class to results. Many people do not like this but it is still part of our culture. In coaching sessions feelings can come to the surface and you need to be able to handle such situations. In counselling sessions very strong feelings can surface by the very nature of counselling.

They may feel that they cannot actually do the task or they may fear for their safety while doing it. In such cases you are challenging them close to the base of Maslow's hierarchy of needs. They may have personal feelings about some of the other people involved, possibly a personality clash or liking or not liking someone. These and other feelings are important as they affect the motivation to do the task and may affect the standard of work achieved.

We are not used to dealing with other people's feelings at work. If people get emotional we get embarrassed. It is as if we have never been emotional ourselves. If people cry we say they 'broke down' as if they are a machine that needs repairing.

When using delegation and coaching it is important to notice if people are not happy about what is happening. Do not get so involved in your own part that you fail to notice their anxiety. Ask simple questions such as:

- ❑ How do you feel about that?
- ❑ Does that seem OK to you?
- ❑ You seem a bit wary of that.
- ❑ I get the feeling that you are a bit worried about it.

Recognize that they may be anxious about doing a task that you take for granted. Give them the opportunity to express their feelings and treat those feelings with respect, not repeating their words to others later. Provide the encouragement and praise they need to build their confidence.

Action

In this chapter we have looked at twelve important aspects that we have loosely called techniques. All these areas are important if you want to be very successful at delegation and coaching. It is certain that you will benefit from improving your skills in some, perhaps many, of these areas.

As a start select three of these twelve areas for improvement. Within each of these three areas select three separate aspects that you will concentrate on to improve. Write these down as objectives or targets.

That gives you nine personal improvement objectives, which is rather a lot. Prioritize these nine and take your top four for the moment. Set deadlines for each of these four and be sure to meet them. After you have achieved them, go back to the others.

10

TWELVE RULES OF THUMB

Use these twelve rules of thumb as a general purpose guide:

1. Spot opportunities

Always be on the lookout for opportunities to coach staff and to delegate tasks that will help them to develop and save time for you. To begin with you will need to think carefully about each step you are taking and devote time and effort to getting it right. In time, as you improve at these skills, the process will come more naturally. Your ultimate aim is to be able to delegate and coach so automatically that both you and your staff cease to think of delegation and coaching as anything special. 'It is just the way we do things around here.'

2. Total understanding of expectations

Always try to ensure that there is complete understanding of what you are asking people to do: the expected outcomes, the limits you are imposing and the authority you are delegating. If they do not understand, you cannot expect them to do it right.

3. Complete tasks

Delegate complete tasks, not bits. If a project is large then different parts, complete in themselves, can be delegated to different people as a team effort. Delegation is about giving them the responsibility to complete the job successfully without grabbing it back for a while.

4. Involve and inform

The process of change requires you to inform your staff and keep them involved if you want their co-operation and commitment. Think of this as seeing eye-to-eye: 'I' for involvement and 'I' for information. But it is eye-to-eye co-operation, as in both looking together at the distant goal, not eye-to-eye confrontation.

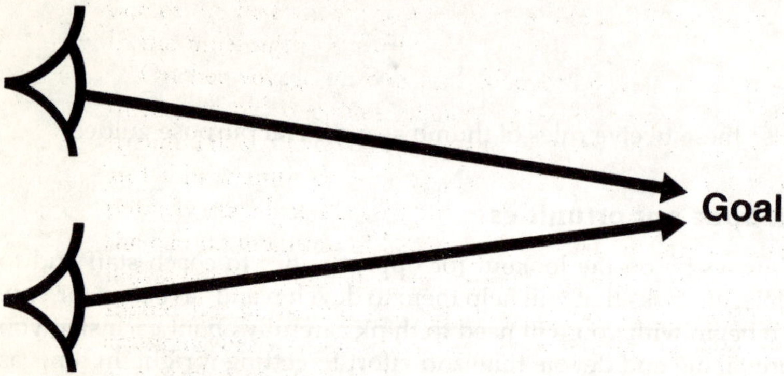

Figure 10.1 *Seeing eye-to-eye*

5. Let them do it

Resist the temptation to interfere and do it yourself. If you are going to do it yourself after all then it is better not to delegate it in the first place. Taking back a delegated task only leads to resentment and hurt pride. 'They obviously think I can't do it.' Only take back a task in an emergency or if you are delegating a bigger one, and then only to help them to free enough of their time to complete the new one in the time allowed.

6. Use for motivation

Give the task of organizing the barrack room to the one who complains most about its organization. Give him or her the challenge and responsibility of solving the puzzle rather than keep on tolerating moans and groans. Delegation and coaching are wonderful motivators. Use them as such and raise the standards of commitment, skill, enthusiasm and achievement throughout your team.

7. Allow mistakes to learn from, but prevent disasters

No one is perfect, we all make mistakes, but with good monitoring, including the safety net of stop points and with honest feedback, there need be no disasters. Engender a culture that treats mistakes as an opportunity to learn, not an opportunity to blame. Remember the saying that, 'Anyone who never made a mistake never did anything.'

8. Praise in public, reprimand in private

Praise is one of the greatest rewards of all and it is a strong motivator. The positive effects of praise can be doubled if others are aware of it, so praise in public but reprimand in private, as the saying goes. Better not to reprimand at all. If you are doing your monitoring job well there should be no call for reprimands, although there may well be times for mutual problem-solving.

9. Say 'Thank you'

Make your people aware that you know about and understand the effort and work they do. Recognize that while results are what your organization and you need from everyone, including yourself, there is enormous striving and effort involved even when the results fall short. Be genuine in your thanks, especially when effort has been great and results not so great. That is when they most need your thanks.

10. Respect them as people

We are all unique and you do not know everything, still less do you know everything about your staff, even people you have known for years. Learn what unexpected talents your people possess. Use those talents to look at things from new angles, to generate new ideas, to solve old problems, and collectively to resolve difficulties you find hard to unlock alone. See your people as unique individuals who together with you make a great team.

11. Complete the cycle

Encourage yourself and your team to progress right round the Kolb Learning Cycle rather than stopping after stage 1, the experience. Reflect on your experiences, learn from them and plan for improvement. Generalize the learning to other areas whenever you can. Learn so as to improve, not so as to cope.

12. Live Theory Y

Let Theory Y be your guide. Catch yourself and stop when you notice yourself slipping into a Theory X approach. Give your staff good jobs to do and expect them to do them well. Treat them as responsible and mature adults who bring their brains to work and want to make their own unique contributions alongside you. Share your work and authority with them, holding them responsible for their actions just as you are for yours.

Further Reading

Adair, J (1979) *Action-centred Leadership*, Gower, Aldershot

Argyris, C (1964) *Integrating the Individual and the Organization*, Wiley, New York

Covey, S R (1992) *The Seven Habits of Highly Effective People*, Simon & Schuster, London

Exodus, Chapter 18, *Good News Bible* (1976) Collins, Glasgow

Herzberg, F, Mausner, B and Synderman, B B (1959) *The Motivation to Work*, 2nd edn, Chapman and Hall, London

Herzberg, F (1968) *Work and the Nature of Man*, Staples Press, London

Honey, P and Mumford, A (1982, rev 1992) *Manual of Learning Styles*, P Honey, Maidenhead

Kennedy, G, Benson, J and McMillan, J (1980) *Managing Negotiations*, 3rd edn, Hutchinson, London

Kolb, D A (1984) *Experiential Learning: Experience as the source of learning and development*, Prentice-Hall, New Jersey

Landsberg, M (1996) *The Tao of Coaching*, HarperCollins, London

Maslow, A H (1943) A theory of human motivation, *Psychological Review*, **50**, pp 370–96

Maslow, A H (1987) *Motivation and Personality*, 3rd edn, Harper and Row, London and New York

McGregor, D (1985) *The Human Side of Enterprise*, McGraw-Hill, New York

Mullins, L J (1996) *Management and Organizational Behaviour*, 4th edn, Pitman Publishing, London

Whitmore, J (1996) *Coaching for Performance*, Nicholas Brealey, London

INDEX